Level 2 • Book 1

Sharing Stories

●

Kindness

●

Look Again

SRA

OPEN COURT READING

Level 2 • Book 1

— PROGRAM AUTHORS —

Carl Bereiter

Marilyn Jager Adams

Marlene Scardamalia

Marcy Stein

Michael Pressley

Marsha Roit

Jan Hirshberg

Anne McKeough

Joe Campione

Iva Carruthers

Gerald H. Treadway, Jr.

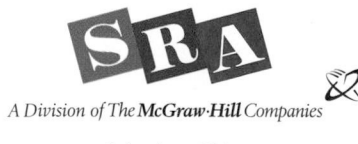

SRA

A Division of The McGraw·Hill Companies

Columbus, Ohio

Acknowledgments

Grateful acknowledgement is given to the following publishers and copyright owners for permissions granted to reprint selections from their publications. All possible care has been taken to trace ownership and secure permission for each selection included. In case of any errors or omissions, the Publisher will be pleased to make suitable acknowledgements in future editions.

SHARING STORIES

"Ant and the Three Little Figs" from MY BROTHER, ANT by Betsy Byars, text copyright © 1996 by Betsy Byars. Used by permission of Viking Penguin, an imprint of Penguin Putnam Books for Young Readers, a division of Penguin Putnam, Inc. "Ant and the Three Little Figs" from MY BROTHER, ANT by Betsy Byars, illustrated by Marc Simont, copyright © 1996 by Marc Simont. Used by permission of Viking Penguin, an imprint of Penguin Putnam Books for Young Readers, a division of Penguin Putnam, Inc.

"Books to the Ceiling" from WHISKERS AND RHYMES by Arnold Lobel. COPYRIGHT © 1985 BY ARNOLD LOBEL. Used by permission of HarperCollins Publishers.

COME BACK, JACK! Copyright © 1993 Catherine and Laurence Anholt. Reproduced by permission of Candlewick Press Inc., Cambridge, MA, on behalf of Walker Books Ltd., London.

"My Book" from Somebody Catch My Homework by David L. Harrison. Text copyright © 1993 by David L. Harrison. Published by Boyds Mills Press, Inc. Reprinted by permission.

THE LIBRARY by Sarah Stewart, illustrated by David Small. Text copyright © 1995 by Sarah Stewart. Illustrations copyright © 1995 by David Small. Reprinted by permission of Farrar, Straus & Giroux, LLC.

STORY HOUR-STARRING MEGAN! text and illustrations © 1992 by Julie Brillhart. Reprinted by permission of the author.

TOMÁS AND THE LIBRARY LADY text copyright © 1997 by Pat Mora. Illustrations copyright © 1997 by Raul Colón. Reprinted by arrangement with Random House Children's Books, a division of Random House, Inc., New York, New York. All rights reserved.

www.sra4kids.com

KINDNESS

From MUSHROOM IN THE RAIN. Text copyright © 1974 by Mirra Ginsburg. Copyright renewed © 2002 by Mirra Ginsburg. Illustrations © 1974 by José Aruego and Ariane Dewey. Illustrations copyright renewed © 2002 by José Aruego and Ariane Dewey. Reproduced by arrangement with Simon & Schuster Books for Young Readers, Simon & Schuster Children's Publishing Division. All rights reserved.

From THE ELVES AND SHOEMAKER by Freya Littledale, illustrated by Brinton Turkle. Text copyright ©1975 by Freya Littledale, illustrations copyright © 1975 by Brinton Turkle. Reprinted by permission of Scholastic, Inc.

THE PAPER CRANE TEXT COPYRIGHT © 1985 BY MOLLY BANG. Used by permission of HarperCollins Publishers.

From BUTTERFLY HOUSE by Eve Bunting, illustrated by Greg Shed. Published by Scholastic Press, a division of Scholastic Inc. Text copyright © 1999 by Edward D. Bunting and Anne E. Bunting Family Trust, illustrations copyright © 1999 by Greg Shed. Reprinted by permission.

From CORDUROY by Don Freeman, copyright © 1968 by Don Freeman. Used by permission of Viking Penguin, an imprint of Penguin Putnam Books for Young Readers, a division of Penguin Putnam Inc.

"April Medicine" from GINGERBREAD DAYS by Joyce Carol Thomas. TEXT COPYRIGHT © 1995 BY JOYCE CAROL THOMAS. ILLUSTRATIONS COPYRIGHT © 1995 BY FLOYD COOPER. Used by permission of HarperCollins Publishers.

From THE STORY OF THREE WHALES Text © Copyright 1998 by Giles Whittell; Illustrations © 1998 by Patrick Benson. Reproduced by permission of Candlewick Press Inc., Cambridge, MA, on behalf of Walker Books Ltd., London.

From CINDERELLA, text copyright © 1977 by Charles Perrault. Reprinted with permission of Flammarion. All rights reserved.

LOOK AGAIN

From I SEE ANIMALS HIDING by Jim Arnosky. Copyright © 1995 by Jim Arnosky. Reprinted by permission of Scholastic Inc.

THEY THOUGHT THEY SAW HIM TEXT COPYRIGHT © 1996 BY CRAIG KEE STRETE. ILLUSTRATIONS COPYRIGHT © 1996 BY JOSÉ ARUEGO AND ARIANE DEWEY. Used by permission of HarperCollins Publishers.

"The Chameleon" from A CHILD'S BESTIARY. Copyright © 1977 by John Gardner. Reprinted by permission of Georges Borchardt, Inc. for the author.

From HUNGRY LITTLE HARE, text copyright © 1998 by Howard Goldsmith, illustrations copyright © 1998 by Denny Bond. Reprinted with permission of Learning Triangle Press, an imprint of The McGraw-Hill Companies. All rights reserved.

From HOW TO HIDE AN OCTOPUS & OTHER SEA CREATURES by Ruth Heller, copyright © 1985. Used by permission of Grosset & Dunlap, A division of Penguin Young Readers Group, A Member of Penguin Group (USA) Inc., 345 Hudson Street, New York, NY 10014. All rights reserved.

HOW THE GUINEA FOWL GOT HER SPOTS by Barbara Knutson. Copyright 1990 by Barbara Knutson. Published by Carolrhoda Books, Inc. a division of the Lerner Publishing Group. Used by permission of the publisher. All rights reserved.

Animal Camouflage by Janet McDonnell, copyright 1998 © by The Child's World ®, Chanhassen Minnesota. Reprinted by permission of copyright holder.

SRA/McGraw-Hill

A Division of The McGraw·Hill Companies

— Program Authors —

Carl Bereiter, Ph.D.
University of Toronto

Marilyn Jager Adams, Ph.D.
BBN Technologies

Michael Pressley, Ph.D.
Michigan State University

Marsha Roit, Ph.D.
National Reading Consultant

Anne McKeough, Ph.D.
University of Toronto

Jan Hirshberg, Ed.D.
Reading Specialist

Marlene Scardamalia, Ph.D.
University of Calgary

Joe Campione, Ph.D.
University of California, Berkeley

Iva Carruthers, Ph.D.
Northeastern Illinois University

Gerald H. Treadway, Jr., Ed.D.
San Diego State University

Marcy Stein, Ph.D.
University of Washington, Tacoma

Table of Contents

Table of Contents

Table of Contents

Sharing Stories

How do you share stories with your friends? What if they are too far away to talk to? Do you write to them? How can you learn new stories? Reading and writing can help us share stories with others.

Stories for Young Readers

13

Ant and the Three Little Figs

Betsy Byars
illustrated by Marc Simont

Ant said, "Read me a story."

I like to read.

I said, "Okay."

Ant sat down by me.

I opened the book

and began to read.

"Once upon a time

there were three little figs."

Ant sat up.

He said, "No! That is not right.

It's pigs. Three little PIGS.

Say PIGS."

I am easy to get along with.

I said, "Pigs."

The Ant leaned back.

He said, "Now read the story."

I read: "Once upon a time

there were three little bananas."

Ant said, "No! Don't do that!

Read the story right.

It's pigs.

Look at the picture.

There's a pig.

There's a pig.

There's a pig.

Three pigs!"

"Oh, all right. Pigs.

Once upon a time

there were three little—"

"Pigs," Ant said quickly.

"Who is reading this—

you or me?" I asked.

"You are," Ant said,

"but you have to say pigs."

"And you have to let me read.

Once upon a time

there were three little—"

I stopped and waited.

The Ant waited, too.

Finally he said,

"This is your last chance.

If you don't say pigs, I'm leaving."

I said, "Oh, all right.

Once upon a time

there were three little pigs. . . ."

Ant got down from the chair.

I said, "Where are you going, Ant?

I read it right. I said pigs."

Ant said, "I am going outside."

"Why, Ant?"

"I don't like the rest of the story.

It has a big bad wolf in it."

I said, "I could change that, Ant.

I could make him a big bad lemon.

Or how about a big bad watermelon?"

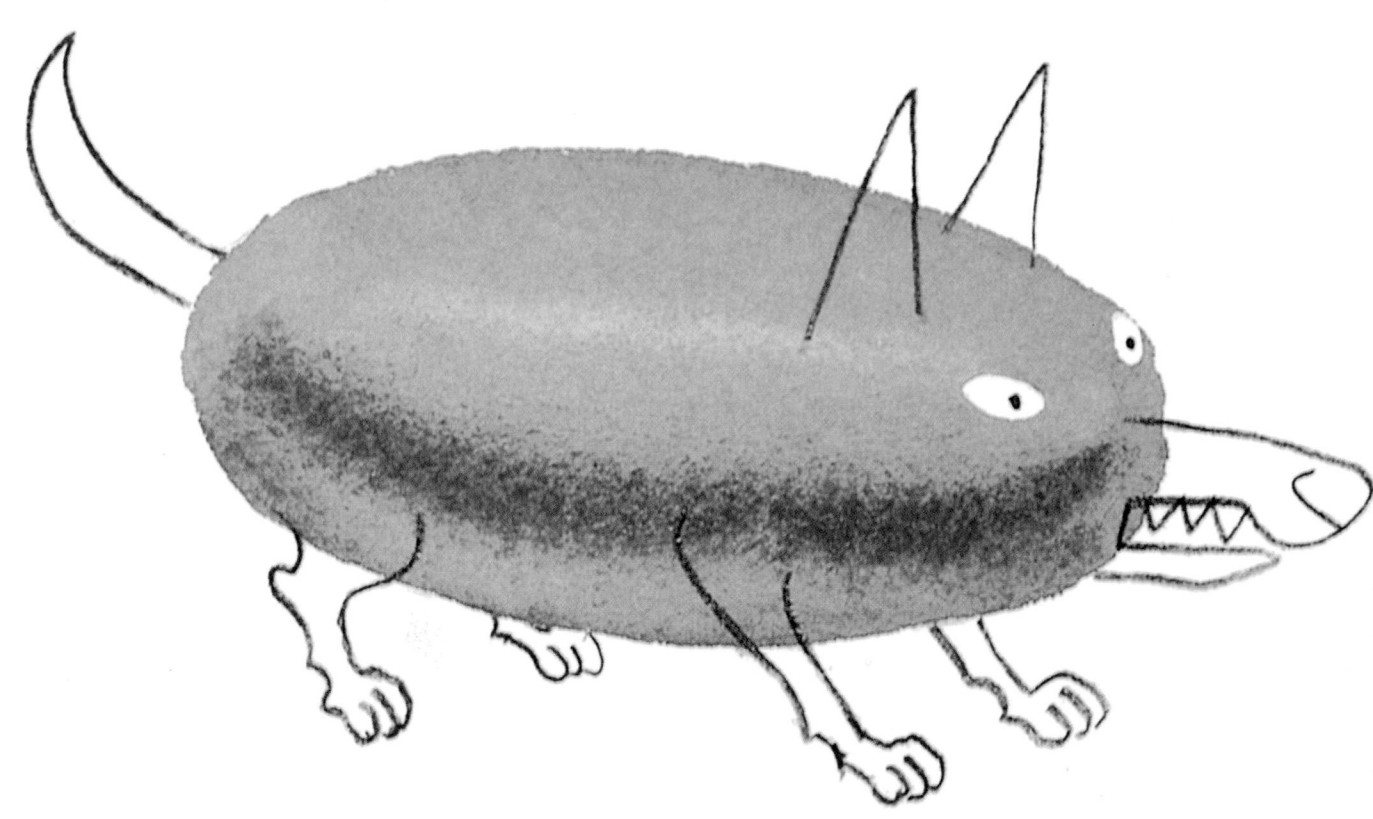

"No," said Ant,

"I would know it was a wolf."

Ant went to the door and opened it.

He looked back at me.

He said, "But thank you

for reading to me."

"You are welcome, Ant,"

I said, "anytime."

Ant and the Three Little Figs

Concept Connections

Linking the Selection

Answer these questions in the Response Journal section of your Writer's Notebook.

- How did Ant's big brother share the story "The Three Little Pigs"?

- Why didn't Ant's brother just share the story as it was in the book?

Exploring Concept Vocabulary

The concept word for this lesson is *imagination.* If you do not know what this word means, look it up in the dictionary. Answer these questions:

- What does *imagination* have to do with sharing stories?

- Which brother showed more *imagination* in this story? Why?

Complete the following sentence with a selection vocabulary word.

It took *imagination* to change pigs to

_____.

Expanding the Concept

Think about "Ant and the Three Little Figs."
What did you learn about sharing stories?

Try to use the word *imagination* as you talk
about this story. Then add new ideas about
sharing stories to the Concept/Question Board.

Meet the Author

Betsy Byars remembers her father
changing certain parts of a story as he read
it to her when she was young. This made her
look closely at the written word. She always
loved books, but she did not start writing
books until her children were teenagers.
She said, *"In that, writing is like baseball
or piano playing. You have got to practice
if you want to be successful."*

Meet the Illustrator

Marc Simont was born in Paris, France.
Because his parents traveled a lot, he
became very skillful at looking closely at
the things around him. As a child he taught
himself to draw by studying a picture book.
He painted portraits and drew illustrations
for advertisements before he became an
illustrator for children's books. *"I believe
that if I like the drawings I do, children
will like them also,"* he said.

Books to the Ceiling

by Arnold Lobel

Books to the ceiling,
books to the sky.
My piles of books are
   a mile high.
How I love them!
How I need them!
I'll have a long beard by
   the time I read them.

Focus Questions Have you ever shared a story with someone younger? In what ways can books be exciting?

Come Back, Jack!

by Catherine and Laurence Anholt

There was once a little girl who didn't like books. Her mom liked books. Her dad liked books. Her brother, Jack, *loved* books, and he couldn't even read.

"Books are boring," the little girl said. And she went out into the yard to find a real adventure.

"Keep an eye on Jack!" called the little girl's mother as Jack sat down with his book on the grass.

The little girl searched for something
exciting in the garden. She didn't find much.
When she turned around, Jack wasn't
looking at his book . . .

. . . he was crawling *inside* it!

"Come back, Jack!" called the little girl.

But Jack was already gone.

She crawled in after him.

Inside the book was a steep green hill, and
at the bottom someone was crying.

"Oh no, he's hurt himself!" said the little
girl.

But it wasn't Jack crying at the bottom of the hill. It was Jill.

"Jack fell down—and now he's run away," Jill said.

"Oh dear!" said the little girl. "Come back, Jack!"

The little girl hadn't gone far when she saw
a strange crowd standing outside a house.

"This is the house that Jack built," said a
cow with a crumpled horn.

"Jack isn't old enough to build houses,"
said the little girl. "He can't even read yet."

"But he's a clever lad," said the cow. "Nimble and quick, too. Just watch him jump over that candlestick!"

"Oh dear," said the little girl . . .

"COME BACK, JACK!"

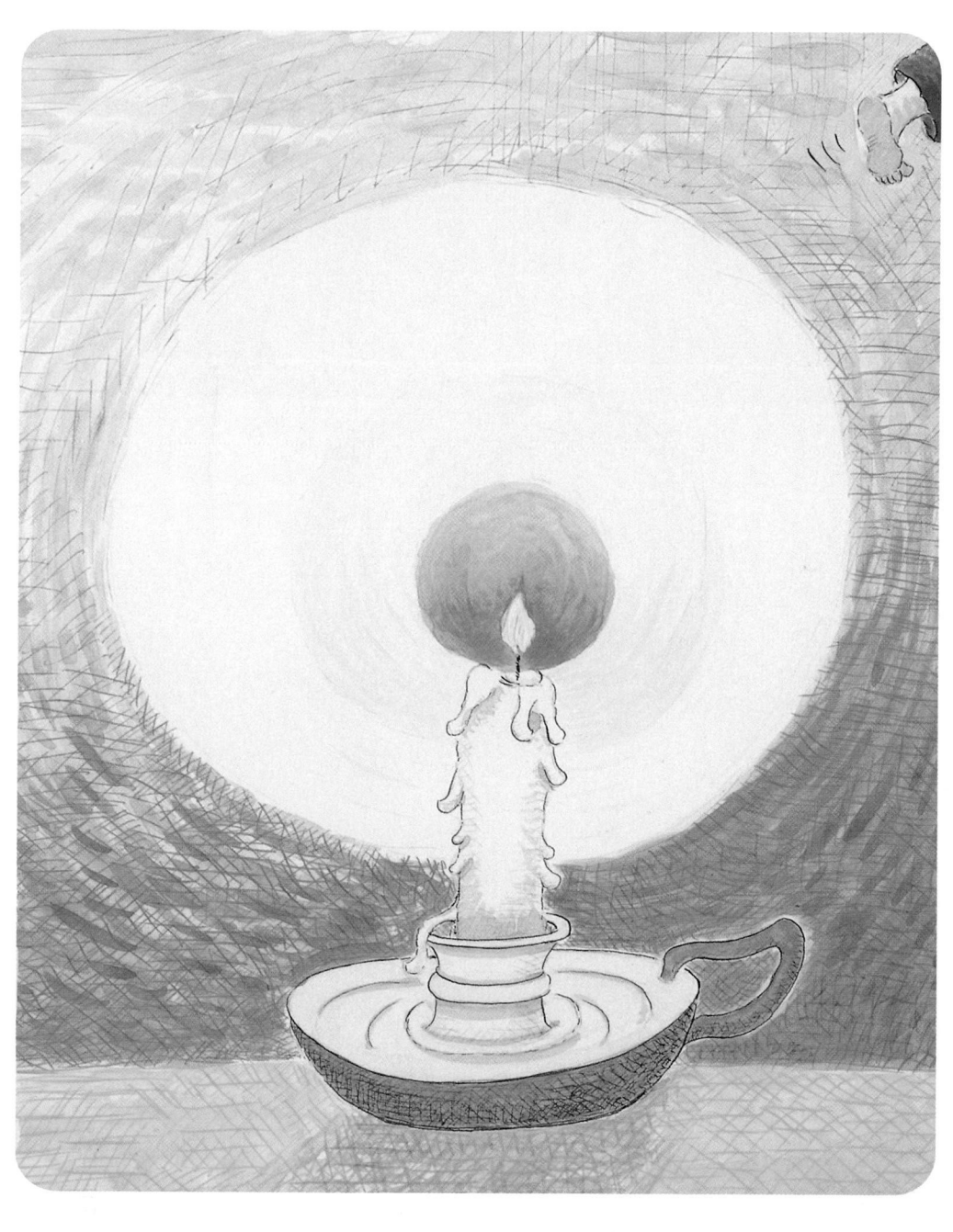

The little girl found herself up in the clouds. She couldn't see Jack. What she could see was a huge castle with its enormous door wide open.

The little girl crept through the castle door—and there was Jack, sitting in a corner, eating a Christmas pie. She was just about to tell him to take out his thumb and eat politely, when the whole castle began to shake.

A great voice roared:

"FEE FI FO FUM,
I'D REALLY LIKE TO
EAT SOMEONE!"

The little girl took hold of Jack's hand, and they ran out of the castle as quickly as they could. But the giant had seen them.

"FUM FO FEE FI, I WANT THOSE CHILDREN IN A PIE!"

Just in time, they found a beanstalk
growing up through the clouds. They started
to climb down it, but the giant was getting
closer. He was about to grab them when . . .

. . . they reached the end of the book and tumbled out into their very own backyard.

The giant's huge, hairy hand stretched out after them, but Jack banged the book shut.

From inside the book came a faraway roar:

"FEE FI FO FUM,
NOW I'VE GONE AND HURT
MY THUMB!"

"Well," said the little girl, "perhaps books aren't boring after all!"

Then she and Jack lay on the grass, and they laughed and laughed and laughed.

Come Back, Jack!

Concept Connections

Linking the Selection

Writer's Notebook — Answer these questions in the Response Journal section of your Writer's Notebook.

- How did Jack share stories with his big sister?

- Jack's sister was looking for an adventure outside in the yard. What kind of adventure did she find instead?

Exploring Concept Vocabulary

The concept word for this lesson is *fantasy*. If you do not know what this word means, look it up in the dictionary. Answer these questions:

- How can you tell this story is a *fantasy?*

- Name another story you have read that is a *fantasy.*

In the Vocabulary section of your Writer's Notebook, write and complete the following sentence using one of the selection vocabulary words.

This *fantasy* is about two children who _____.

Expanding the Concept

Think about "Ant and the Three Little Figs" and "Come Back, Jack!" What did you learn about sharing stories?

Try to use the word *fantasy* as you talk about the characters and their actions in these stories. Then add new ideas about sharing stories to the Concept/Question Board.

Meet the Author and the Illustrator

Catherine and Laurence Anholt were both born in London, England. They were married in 1984 and soon after began to work together to create their own books. He usually writes the stories and she illustrates them. They want children to see themselves in the stories and to enjoy reading them.

Laurence Anholt first worked as an art teacher and wrote children's books in his free time. Many of his ideas came from listening to his three children talking. *"I want children to get the message that books are fun—it is okay to enjoy yourself."* Catherine Anholt said, *"All my drawings are from memory, although I have always intended to work from life."*

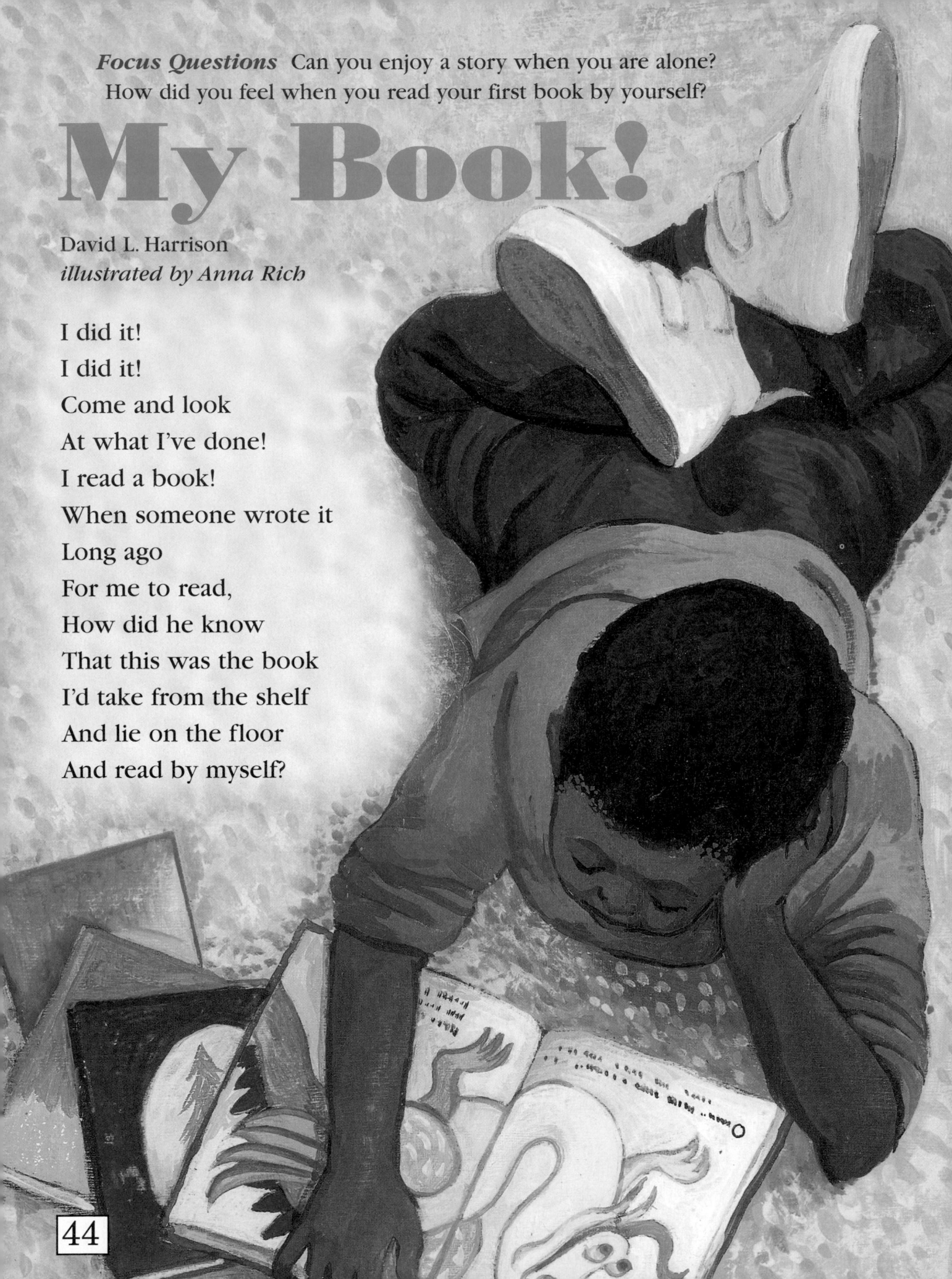

My Book!

David L. Harrison
illustrated by Anna Rich

I did it!
I did it!
Come and look
At what I've done!
I read a book!
When someone wrote it
Long ago
For me to read,
How did he know
That this was the book
I'd take from the shelf
And lie on the floor
And read by myself?

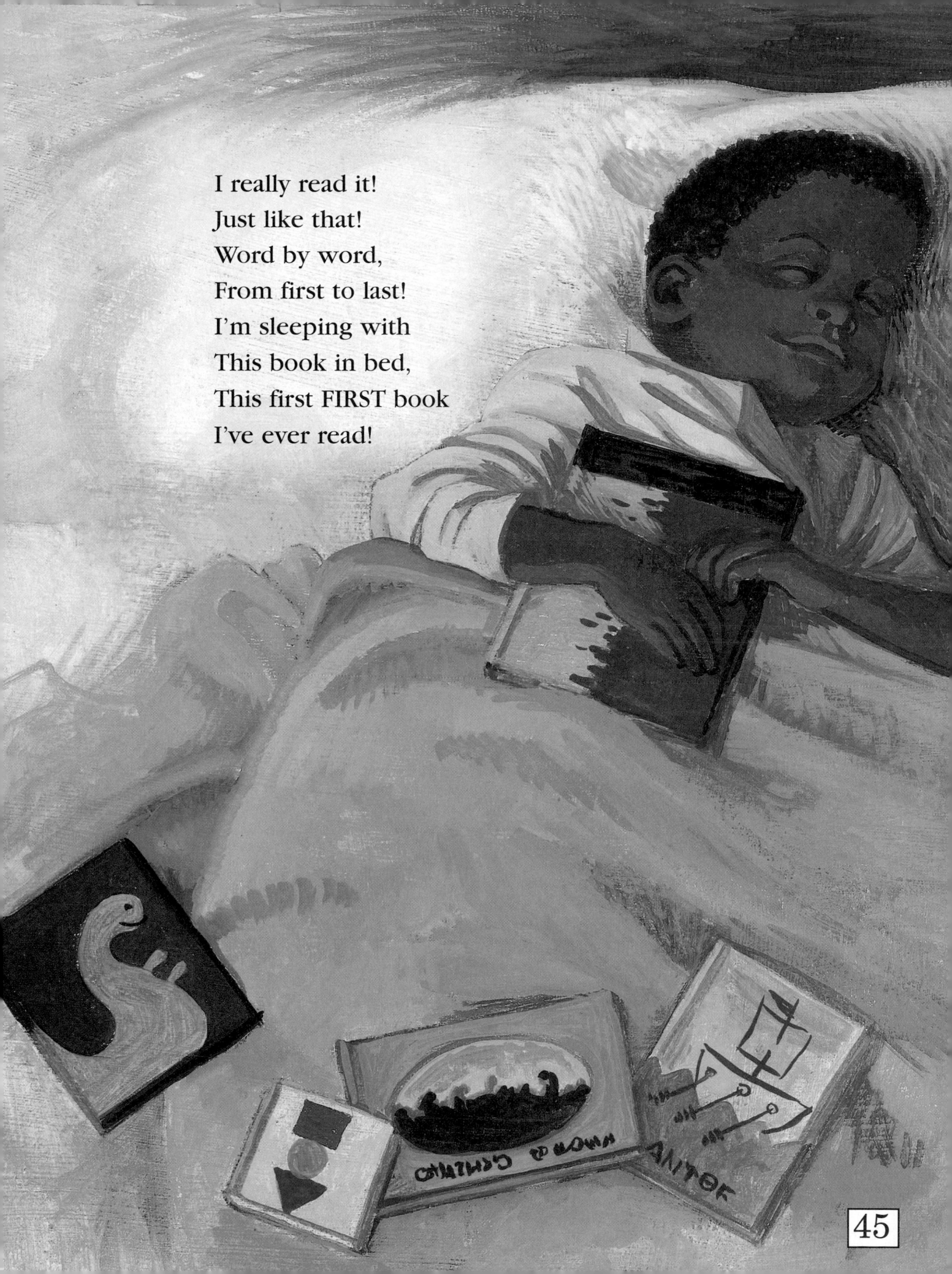

I really read it!
Just like that!
Word by word,
From first to last!
I'm sleeping with
This book in bed,
This first FIRST book
I've ever read!

45

THE Library

Sarah Stewart
illustrated by David Small

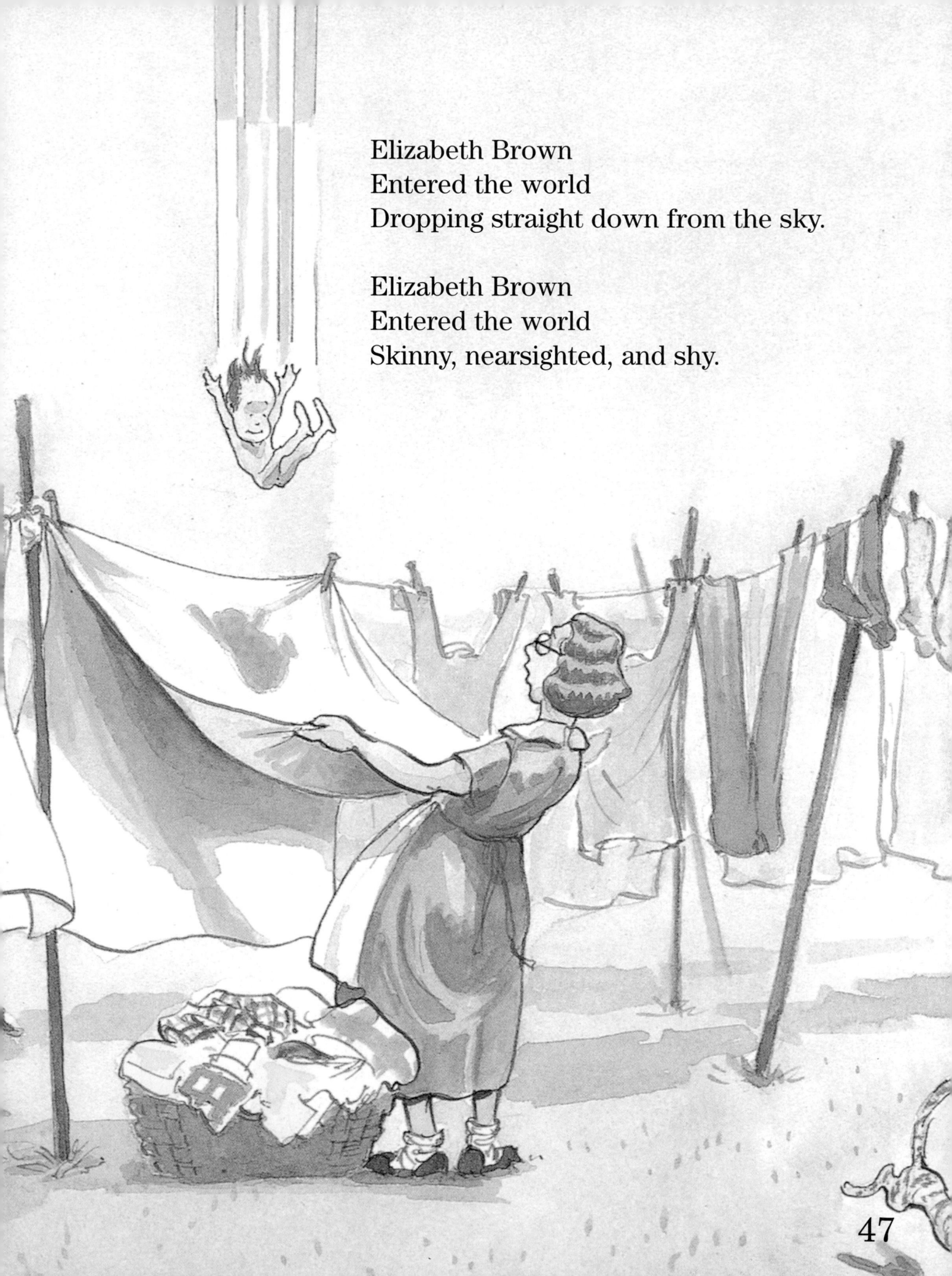

Elizabeth Brown
Entered the world
Dropping straight down from the sky.

Elizabeth Brown
Entered the world
Skinny, nearsighted, and shy.

47

She didn't like to play with dolls,
She didn't like to skate.
She learned to read quite early
And at an incredible rate.

She always took a book to bed,
With a flashlight under the sheet.
She'd make a tent of covers
And read herself to sleep.

Elizabeth Brown
Went off to school
Dragging a steamer trunk.

Elizabeth Brown
Unpacked her books,
Breaking the upper bunk.

She sat in all her classes
And doodled on a pad,
Adrift in dreams of entering
A readers' olympiad.

She manufactured library cards
And checked out books to friends,
Then shocked them with her midnight raids
To collect the books again.

Elizabeth Brown
Preferred a book
To going on a date.

While friends went out
And danced till dawn,
She stayed up reading late.

51

She took the train one afternoon
And promptly lost her way,
So bought a house and settled down
To tutoring for pay.

Elizabeth Brown
Walked into town
Summer, fall, winter, and spring.

Elizabeth Brown
Walked into town
Looking for only one thing.

She didn't want potato chips,
She didn't want new clothes.
She went straight to the bookstore.
"May I have one of **those**?"

Elizabeth Brown
Walked right back home
And read and read and read.

She even read while
Exercising,
And standing on her head.

She made a list of groceries
And tucked it in her book,
Then lost the list among the fruits
And left with nothing to cook.

She read about Greek goddesses
While vacuuming the floor.
Attending only to her book,
She'd walk into a door.

55

Books were piled on top of chairs
And spread across the floor.
Her shelves began to fall apart,
As she read more and more.

Big books made very solid stacks
On which teacups could rest.
Small books became the building blocks
For busy little guests.

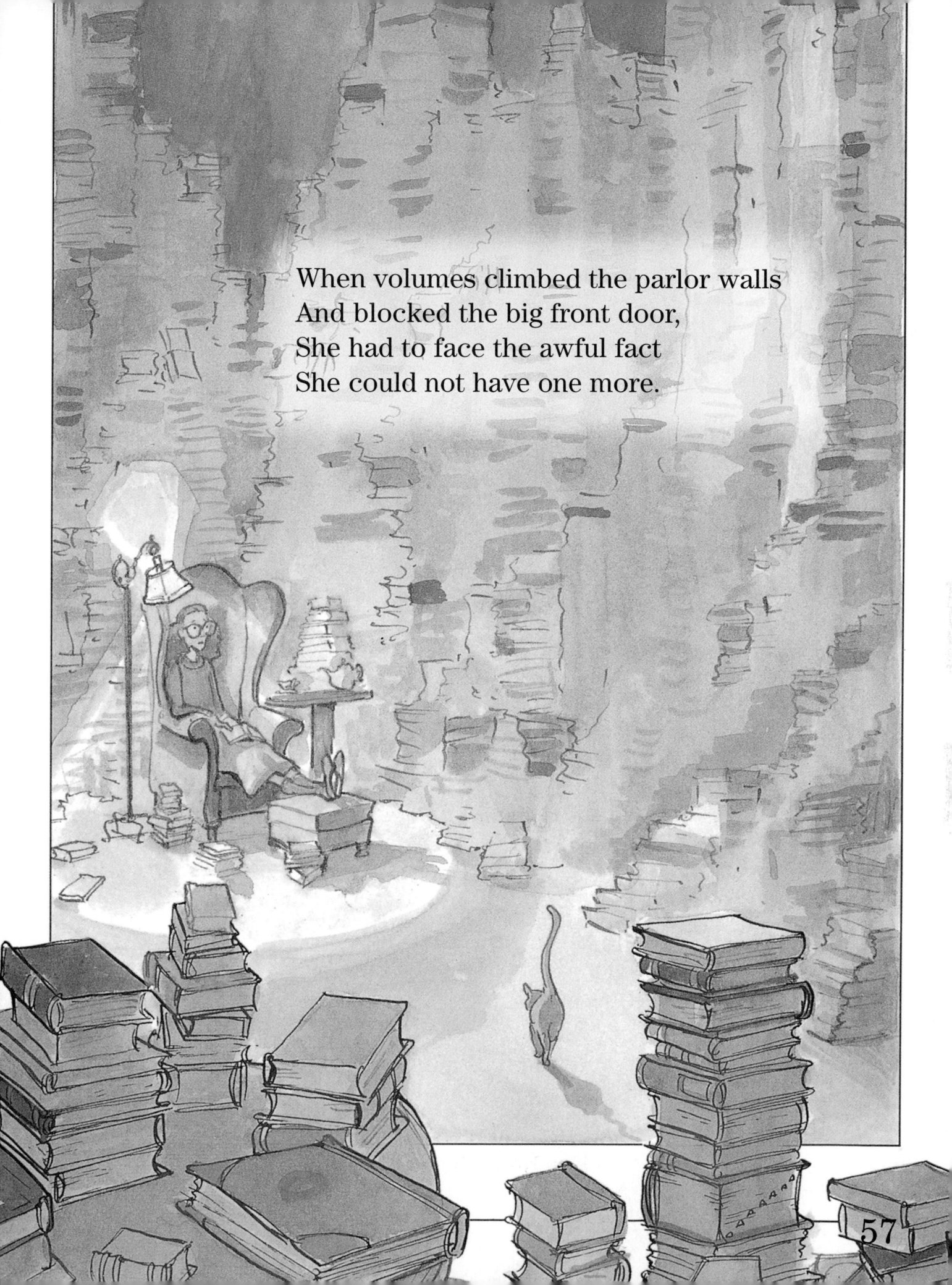

When volumes climbed the parlor walls
And blocked the big front door,
She had to face the awful fact
She could not have one more.

57

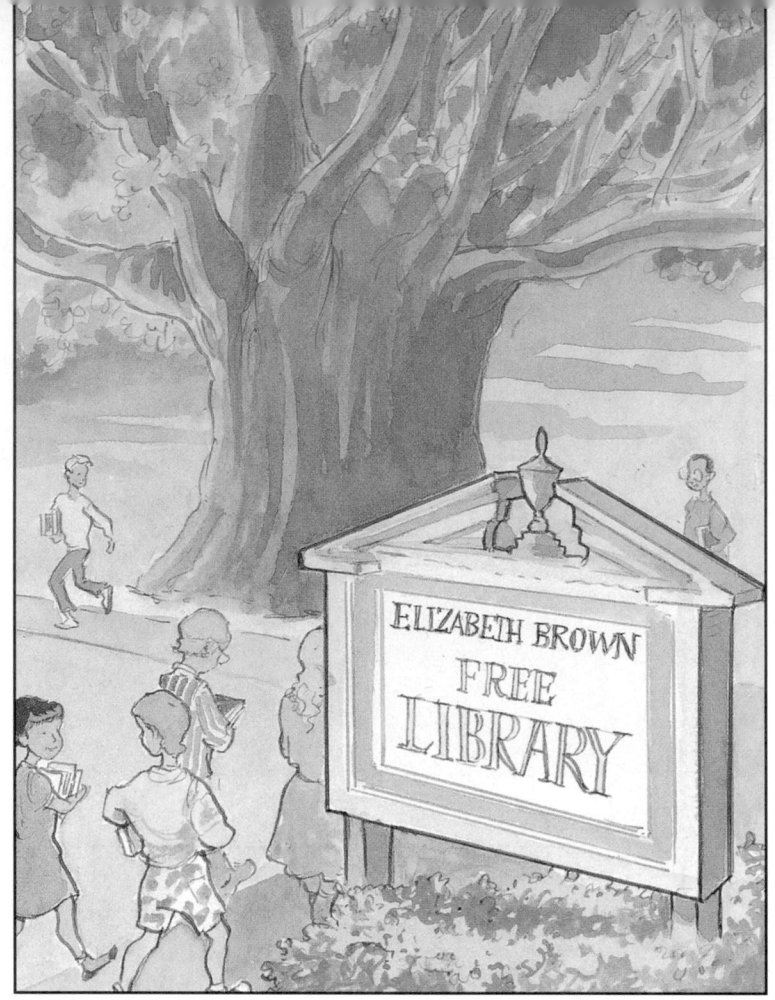

Elizabeth Brown
Walked into town
That very afternoon.

Elizabeth Brown
Walked into town
Whistling a happy tune.

She didn't want a bicycle,
She didn't want silk bows.
She went straight to the courthouse—
"May I have one of **those**?"

The form was for donations.
She quickly wrote this line:
*"I, E. Brown, give to the town
All that was ever mine."*

Elizabeth Brown
Moved in with a friend
And lived to a ripe old age.

They walked to the library
Day after day,
And turned page . . .
after page . . .

after page.

59

THE Library

Concept Connections

Linking the Selection

 Answer these questions in the Response Journal section of your Writer's Notebook.

- Why did Elizabeth Brown have so many books?

- What did Elizabeth decide to do with her books?

Exploring Concept Vocabulary

The concept word for this lesson is *share.* If you do not know what this word means, look it up in the dictionary. Answer these questions:

- How did Elizabeth Brown *share* stories with other people?

- How can you *share* stories with other people?

Complete the following sentence with a selection vocabulary word.

Elizabeth decided to *share* her books, which provided her town with a _____.

60

Expanding the Concept

Think about "The Library" and the other unit selections you have read. What have you learned about sharing stories?

Try to use the word **share** as you talk about the characters and their actions in these stories.

Meet the Author

Sarah Stewart grew up in Texas. While growing up she had two favorite places where she loved to go to listen to the silence and explore the world around her. These two places were her grandmother's garden and the library. Stewart spent many days in these places daydreaming and writing. She now lives in a historic home in Michigan with her husband, her dog Simon, and her cat Otis. She also has three children.

Meet the Illustrator

David Small was born in Detroit, Michigan. His father was a doctor— a radiologist. When David Small was a child he learned to draw pictures of people by looking at their x-rays. Looking at people's skeletons taught him why they move and look the way they do. David Small likes to write books too. *"Of all the things I do as an artist, the creation of children's picture books is the most pleasurable,"* he said. David Small feels like he's putting on a whole show when he writes a book and draws the pictures to go with the words.

Focus Questions Can sharing stories with others make us better readers? Would you enjoy reading to other children during story hour at the library?

Story Hour – Starring Megan!

by Julie Brillhart

Once in awhile, when the sitter couldn't come, Megan and her baby brother, Nathan, got to spend an afternoon with their mother at the town library. Their mother was the librarian.

62

Megan liked the library because she had
jobs to do. Her mother called her the
"assistant." She put away the children's books
and picked up the stuffed animals.

She decorated the bulletin board and watered the plants.

And when things got very, very busy, Megan was always ready to help with Nathan.

But most of all, Megan liked the library because she loved books and was learning to read. She couldn't wait to read every book in the whole library!

Whenever she had a chance, Megan would curl up with *Fly up High* and try to sound out the words. Often she got stuck, and her mother would help her.

Megan would sigh. "Oh, reading is so hard!"

"I know," said her mother. "But keep trying. It will come."

So Megan kept on trying. She tried at school, in the car, at the supermarket, in the bathtub, after dinner, and even after lights out!

She had never tried so hard at anything before.

One time the sitter couldn't come on the day Megan's mother had story hour. "I hope Nathan sleeps through the story," said Megan's mother as the children started to arrive.

Suddenly a stuffed dinosaur came flying through the book slot in the library door. "Oh, good!" said Megan. "Andrew's here!"

Andrew came in carrying a pile of dinosaur books. "Guess what?" said Megan. "I'm learning to read!"

"Oh," said Andrew. "Are there any new books with pteranodons?"

"No," said Megan. "And aren't you ever going to read about *anything* else?"

Megan led the group to the children's room and passed out name tags. She helped the younger children pin on their tags.

"Welcome to story hour," said Megan's mother. "Today I would like to read—"

Right then Nathan let out a howl. Everyone turned to look.

"Just a minute," said Megan's mother. And she got up.

She tried everything to calm Nathan down, but he kept screaming.

The children were getting restless. "Please be patient," said Megan's mother. "I'm sure we will begin shortly."

While all this was going on, Megan sat thinking. Suddenly she had a great idea!

She slipped away and ran to get her favorite book.

Megan sat down in front of all the children. She felt a little scared. "I would like to read *Fly up High*," she said.

Everyone looked at her in amazement. The room became very quiet, and Nathan even stopped crying. Megan began to read.

She read on and on. She showed the
children the pictures, just the way her
mother did. She got stuck on a few words,
but she kept going. Nobody seemed to notice
when she made a mistake.

She read the whole book!

The children all clapped and cheered. And so did some moms and dads who had come in. Megan felt terrific!

She looked over at her mom. "I did it!"
Megan said.

"You sure did," said her mother. "And all by
yourself! I'm very proud of you!"

"I didn't know you could read THAT much," said Andrew. "Can I borrow your book?"

Megan laughed. "Sure," she said. "But it's not about dinosaurs!"

When everyone had gone, Megan's mother gave her a big, big hug. "You were wonderful!" she said. "You saved the day!"

"Yay!" said Megan. "Now I'll read every book in the whole library!"

And she started right away.

Story Hour – Starring Megan!

Concept Connections

Linking the Selection

Writer's Notebook Answer these questions in the Response Journal section of your Writer's Notebook.

• Why did Megan want to learn to read?

• How was Megan able to help her mother?

Exploring Concept Vocabulary

The concept word for this lesson is **storyteller.** If you do not know what this word means, look it up in the dictionary. Answer this question:

• How does a **storyteller** share stories?

In the Vocabulary section of your Writer's Notebook, write a sentence using the word **storyteller** and a selection vocabulary word.

Expanding the Concept

Think about "Story Hour—Starring Megan!" and the other unit selections you have read. What have you learned about sharing stories?

Try to use the word **storyteller** as you talk about the characters and their actions in these stories. Then add new ideas about sharing stories to the Concept/Question Board.

Meet the Author and Illustrator

Julie Brillhart used to work as a librarian before she began writing and illustrating children's books. Many of the ideas for her books came from working with children in the library. She takes everyday moments and turns them into stories and art.

Although her own children are grown, her favorite thing to do is to go to the children's room at her local library. Every week she spends an afternoon picking out children's books to take home and read.

The Library. 1960. **Jacob Lawrence.** Tempera on fiberboard.
60.9 × 75.8 cm. The National Museum of American Art,
Smithsonian Institution, Washington, DC.

***Romans Parisiens.* Vincent van Gogh.** Oil on canvas. Private collection.

Jungle Tales. 1895. **James J. Shannon.** Oil on canvas. 87 × 113.7 cm. The Metropolitan Museum of Art.

Focus Questions Who can be a storyteller?
Does your family tell or read stories to one another?

Tomás and the Library Lady

Pat Mora
illustrated by Raul Colón

It was midnight. The light of the full
moon followed the tired old car. Tomás
was tired too. Hot and tired. He missed his
own bed, in his own house in Texas.

Tomás was on his way to Iowa again with his family. His mother and father were farm workers. They picked fruit and vegetables for Texas farmers in the winter and for Iowa farmers in the summer. Year after year they bump-bumped along in their rusty old car. "Mamá," whispered Tomás, "if I had a glass of cold water, I would drink it in large gulps. I would suck the ice. I would pour the last drops of water on my face."

Tomás was glad when the car finally stopped. He helped his grandfather, Papá Grande, climb down. Tomás said, *"Buenas noches"*—"Good night"—to Papá, Mamá, Papá Grande, and to his little brother, Enrique. He curled up on the cot in the small house that his family shared with the other workers.

Early the next morning Mamá and Papá
went out to pick corn in the green fields. All
day they worked in the hot sun. Tomás and
Enrique carried water to them. Then the
boys played with a ball Mamá had sewn
from an old teddy bear.

When they got hot, they sat under a tree
with Papá Grande. "Tell us the story about
the man in the forest," said Tomás.

Tomás liked to listen to Papá Grande tell
stories in Spanish. Papá Grande was the best
storyteller in the family.

"En un tiempo pasado," Papá Grande began. "Once upon a time . . . on a windy night a man was riding a horse through a forest. The wind was howling, *whooooooooo*, and the leaves were blowing, *whish, whish . . .*

"All of a sudden something grabbed the man. He couldn't move. He was too scared to look around. All night long he wanted to ride away. But he couldn't.

"How the wind howled, *whooooooooo*.
How the leaves blew. How his teeth
chattered!

"Finally the sun came up. Slowly the man
turned around. And who do you think was
holding him?"

Tomás smiled and said, "A thorny tree."

Papá Grande laughed. "Tomás, you know
all my stories," he said. "There are many
more in the library. You are big enough to
go by yourself. Then you can teach us new
stories."

The next morning Tomás walked downtown. He looked at the big library. Its tall windows were like eyes glaring at him. Tomás walked around and around the big building. He saw children coming out carrying books. Slowly he started climbing up, up the steps. He counted them to himself in Spanish. *Uno, dos, tres, cuatro* . . . His mouth felt full of cotton.

Tomás stood in front of the library doors. He pressed his nose against the glass and peeked in. The library was huge!

Softly Tomás said, "I have a sad word to teach you today. The word is *adiós*. It means good-bye."

Tomás was going back to Texas. He would miss this quiet place, the cool water, the many books. He would miss the library lady.

"My mother sent this to thank you," said Tomás, handing her a small package. "It is *pan dulce*, sweet bread. My mother makes the best *pan dulce* in Texas."

The library lady said, "How nice. How very nice. *Gracias*, Tomás. Thank you." She gave Tomás a big hug.

That night, bumping along again in the
tired old car, Tomás held a shiny new book,
a present from the library lady. Papá Grande
smiled and said, "More stories for the new
storyteller."

Tomás closed his eyes. He saw the
dinosaurs drinking cool water long ago. He
heard the cry of the wild snakebird. He felt
the warm neck of the dinosaur as he held on
tight for a bumpy ride.

Tomás and the Library Lady

Concept Connections

Linking the Selection

Writer's Notebook

Answer these questions in the Response Journal section of your Writer's Notebook.

- Why did Tomás decide to go to the library?

- What talent did Tomás and his grandfather share?

Exploring Concept Vocabulary

The concept word for this lesson is **purpose**. If you do not know what this word means, look it up in the dictionary. Answer these questions:

- What was Papá Grande's **purpose** in suggesting that Tomás go to the library?

- What was the library lady's **purpose** in asking Tomás to teach her some Spanish words?

Complete the following sentence with a selection vocabulary word.

Papá Grande's **purpose** was to share a scary story about

_____.

Expanding the Concept

Think about "Tomás and the Library Lady" and the other unit selections. What have you learned about sharing stories?

Try to use the word **purpose** as you talk about these stories. Then add new ideas to the Concept/Question Board.

Meet the Author

Pat Mora's family spoke two languages at home, so she learned to speak and write in both English and Spanish. She was able to use both in her writing, as in "Tomás and the Library Lady." Pat Mora was a teacher for nearly twenty years before she began a career as a writer. She writes poetry and nonfiction, as well as children's literature. *"I've always enjoyed reading all kinds of books and now I get to write them too, to sit and play with words on my computer."*

Meet the Illustrator

Raul Colón dreamed of becoming an artist as a young child. He would hand in his homework with doodles and drawings. He likes to scratch the paper with a special tool before he uses colored pencils. This gives his illustrations a special effect. His work has included puppet designs, album covers, short animated films, and illustrations for children's books.

What does it mean to be kind? Who is kind? How do you know? Stories can help us learn about kindness.

Mushroom in the Rain

retold by Mirra Ginsburg

illustrated by José Aruego and Ariane Dewey

One day an ant was caught in the rain. "Where can I hide?" he wondered.

He saw a tiny mushroom peeking out of the ground in a clearing, and he hid under it. He sat there, waiting for the rain to stop. But the rain came down harder and harder.

108

A wet butterfly crawled up to the mushroom.

"Cousin Ant, let me come in from the rain. I am so wet I cannot fly."

"How can I let you in?" said the ant. "There is barely room enough for one."

"It does not matter," said the butterfly. "Better crowded than wet."

The ant moved over and made room for the butterfly. The rain came down harder and harder.

A mouse ran up.

"Let me in under the mushroom. I am drenched to the bone."

"How can we let you in? There is no more room here."

"Just move a little closer!"

They huddled closer and let the mouse in. And the rain came down and came down and would not stop.

A little sparrow hopped up to the
mushroom, crying: "My feathers are
dripping, my wings are so tired! Let me in
under the mushroom to dry out and rest
until the rain stops!"

"But there is no room here."

"Please! Move over just a little!"

They moved over, and there was room
enough for the sparrow.

Then a rabbit hopped into the clearing and saw the mushroom.

"Oh, hide me!" he cried. "Save me! A fox is chasing me!"

"Poor rabbit," said the ant. "Let's crowd ourselves a little more and take him in."

As soon as they hid the rabbit, the fox
came running.

"Have you seen the rabbit? Which way did
he go?" he asked.

"We have not seen him."

The fox came nearer and sniffed. "There is
a rabbit smell around. Isn't he hiding here?"

"You silly fox! How could a rabbit get in here? Don't you see there isn't any room?"

The fox turned up his nose, flicked his tail, and ran off.

By then the rain was over. The sun looked out from behind the clouds. And everyone came out from under the mushroom, bright and merry.

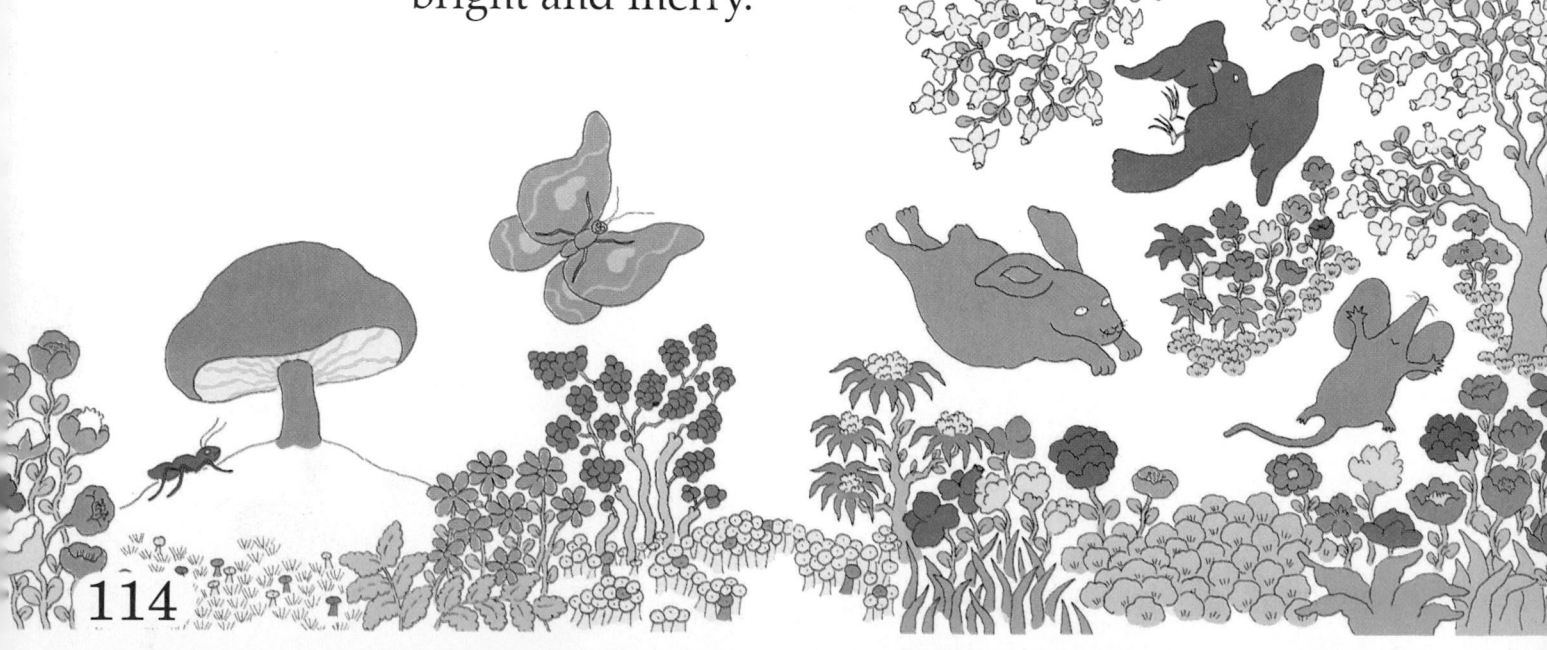

The ant looked at his neighbors. "How could this be? At first I had hardly room enough under the mushroom just for myself, and in the end all five of us were able to sit under it."

"Qua-ha-ha! Qua-ha-ha!" somebody laughed loudly behind them.

They turned and saw a fat green frog sitting on top of the mushroom, shaking his head at them.

"Qua-ha-ha!" said the frog. "Don't you know what happens to a mushroom in the rain?" And he hopped away, still laughing.

The ant, the
butterfly, the mouse,
the sparrow, and the
rabbit looked at one another, then at the
mushroom. And suddenly they knew why
there was room enough under the mushroom
for them all.

Do you know? Can you guess what
happens to a mushroom when it rains?

IT GROWS!

Mushroom in the Rain

Concept Connections

Linking the Selection

Writer's Notebook Answer these questions in the Response Journal section of your Writer's Notebook.

- Why were the animals kind to the rabbit?

- Why weren't the animals kind to the fox?

Exploring Concept Vocabulary

The concept word for this lesson is **sympathy.** If you do not know what this word means, look it up in the dictionary. Answer these questions:

- What does **sympathy** have to do with being kind?

- How did the animals show **sympathy** to the rabbit?

Complete the following sentence with a selection vocabulary word.

The animals expressed kindness and **sympathy** by hiding the rabbit as they all _____.

Expanding the Concept

Think about "Mushroom in the Rain." What did you learn about kindness from this story?

Try to use the word **sympathy** as you talk about the characters and their actions in this story.

Meet the Author

Mirra Ginsburg was born in a small Russian village much like the towns in the folktales that she loved to read. She began writing children's books by taking books written in Russian or Yiddish and rewriting them in English so that American children could enjoy them. Before long, she was making up her own stories. She said, *"From my father, I learned to love animals and green growing things. As a child, I was surrounded with them."*

Meet the Illustrators

José Aruego and Ariane Dewey have combined their talents and have illustrated more than sixty children's books. Mr. Aruego does the drawings and Ms. Dewey adds the color through paint. José Aruego began a career in law, but after a few months he realized that he wanted to draw, not practice law. After graduating from art school, he began drawing cartoons and later began illustrating children's books. Ariane Dewey always loved bright colors. In fourth grade art class, she painted bright pink kids swimming in a blue-green lake. Her love of joyful colors is seen in many children's books.

The Elves and the Shoemaker

retold by Freya Littledale
illustrated by Brinton Turkle

There was once a good shoemaker who became very poor. At last he had only one piece of leather to make one pair of shoes. "Well," said the shoemaker to his wife, "I will cut the leather tonight and make the shoes in the morning."

120

The next morning he went to his table, and he couldn't believe what he saw. The leather was polished. The sewing was done. And there was a fine pair of shoes! Not one stitch was out of place.

"Do you see what I see?" asked the shoemaker.

"Indeed I do," said his wife. "I see a fine pair of shoes."

"But who could have made them?" the shoemaker said.

"It's just like magic!" said his wife.

At that very moment a man came in with a top hat and cane. "Those shoes look right for me," said the man. And so they were. They were right from heel to toe. "How much do they cost?"

"One gold coin," said the shoemaker.

"I'll give you two," said the man.

And he went on his way with a smile on his face and the new shoes on his feet.

"Well, well," said the shoemaker, "now I can buy leather for two pairs of shoes." And he cut the leather that night so he could make the shoes in the morning.

The next morning the shoemaker woke up, and he found two pairs of ladies' shoes. They were shining in the sunlight.

"Who is making these shoes?" said the shoemaker. "They are the best shoes in the world."

At that very moment two ladies came in.
They looked exactly alike. "My, what pretty
shoes!" said the ladies. "They will surely fit
us." And the ladies were right. They gave the
shoemaker four gold coins and away they
went . . . clickety-clack, clickety-clack in
their pretty new shoes.

And so it went. Every night the shoemaker cut the leather. Every morning the shoes were made. And every day more people came to buy his beautiful shoes.

Just before Christmas the shoemaker said, "Whoever is making these shoes is making us very happy."

"And rich," said his wife.

127

"Let us stay up and see who it is," the shoemaker said.

"Good," said his wife. So they hid behind some coats, and they waited and waited and waited. When the clock struck twelve, in came two little elves.

"*Elves*," cried the shoemaker.

"Shh!" said his wife.

At once the elves hopped up on the table and set to work. Tap-tap went their hammers. Snip-snap went their scissors. Stitch-stitch went their needles. Their tiny fingers moved so fast the shoemaker and his wife could hardly believe their eyes.

The elves sewed and they hammered and they didn't stop until all the shoes were finished. There were little shoes and big ones. There were white ones and black ones and brown ones. The elves lined them all in a row. Then they jumped down from the table. They ran across the room and out the door.

The next morning the wife said, "The elves have made us very happy. I want to make them happy too. They need new clothes to keep warm. So I'll make them pants and shirts and coats. And I'll knit them socks and hats. You can make them each a pair of shoes."

"Yes, yes!" said the shoemaker. And they went right to work.

131

The Elves and the Shoemaker

Concept Connections

Linking the Selection

Writer's Notebook Answer these questions in the Response Journal section of your Writer's Notebook.

- How did the poor shoemaker and his wife become rich and successful?

- Do you think the elves expected the shoemaker to return their kindness? Why or why not?

Exploring Concept Vocabulary

The concept word for this lesson is **gratitude.** If you do not know what this word means, look it up in the dictionary. Answer this question:

- How did the shoemaker and his wife show their **gratitude** to the elves?

Complete the following sentence with a selection vocabulary word.

The shoemaker appreciated the elves' kindness and felt **gratitude** because he could sell the _____.

Expanding the Concept

Think about "The Elves and the Shoemaker" and "Mushroom in the Rain." What did you learn about kindness from these stories?

Try to use the word *gratitude* as you talk about these stories. Then add new ideas about kindness to the Concept/Question Board.

Meet the Author

Freya Littledale spent much of her free time as a child reading. She especially enjoyed fairy tales. When she was nine-years old, she began writing her own stories and poems. She always loved writing and retelling stories for children. Littledale kept sharing her stories for the rest of her life.

Meet the Illustrator

Brinton Turkle has added his special magic to more than fifty children's books. *"I find the combination of words and pictures that is possible today only in children's books very exciting . . . children [who] must never be offered less than the very best."*

137

The Paper Crane

by Molly Bang

A man once owned a restaurant on a busy road. He loved to cook good food and he loved to serve it. He worked from morning until night, and he was happy.

138

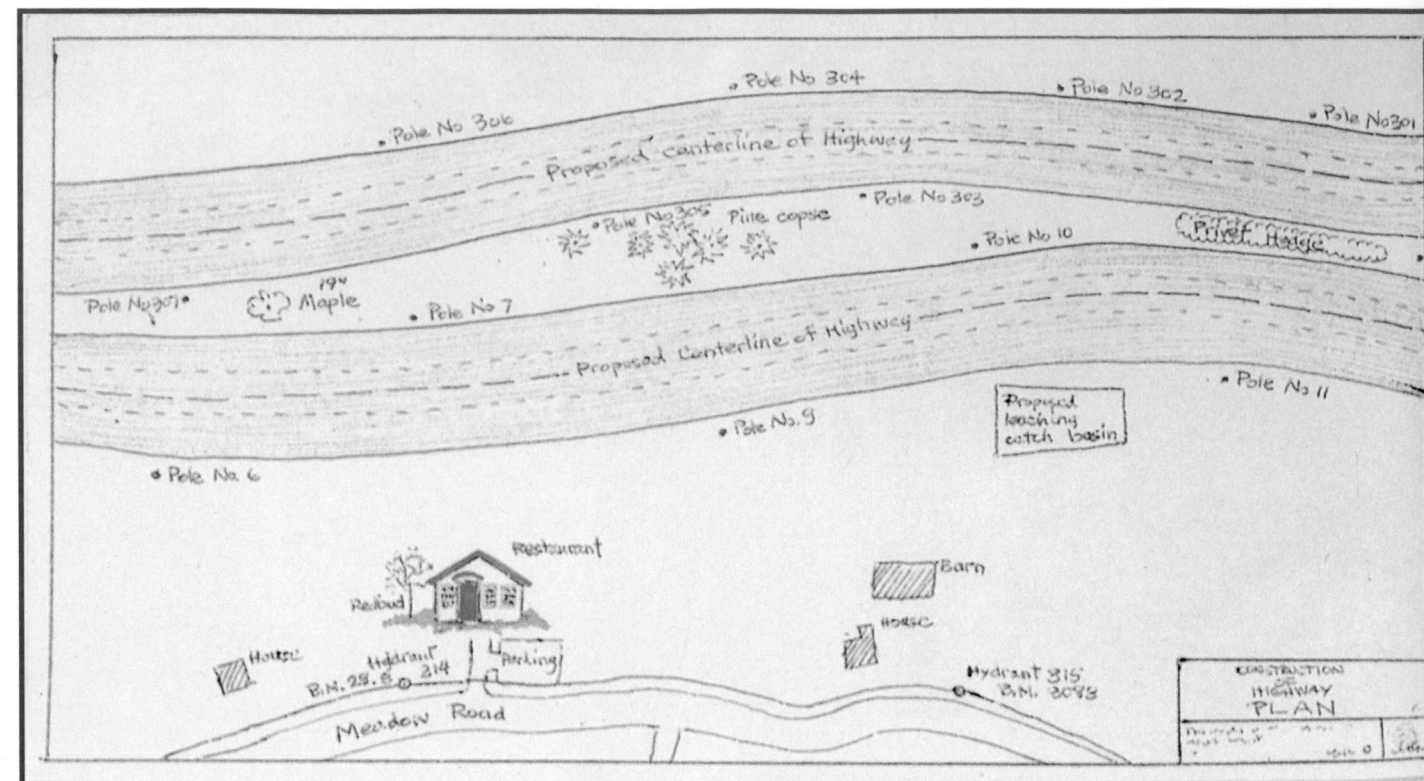

But a new highway was built close by. Travelers drove straight from one place to another and no longer stopped at the restaurant. Many days went by when no guests came at all. The man became very poor, and had nothing to do but dust and polish his empty plates and tables.

140

141

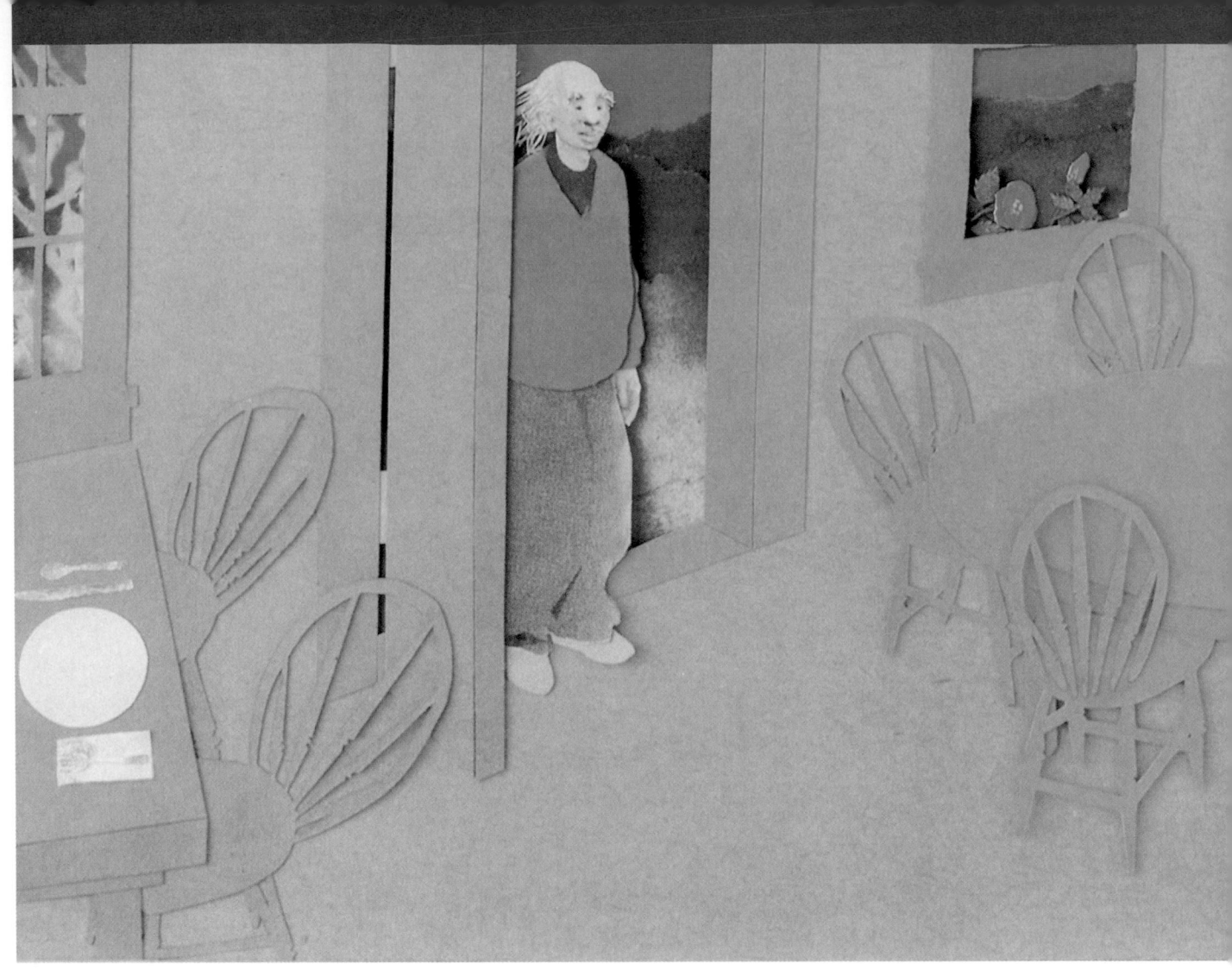

One evening a stranger came into the restaurant. His clothes were old and worn, but he had an unusual, gentle manner.

Though he said he had no money to pay for food, the owner invited him to sit down. He cooked the best meal he could make and served him like a king.

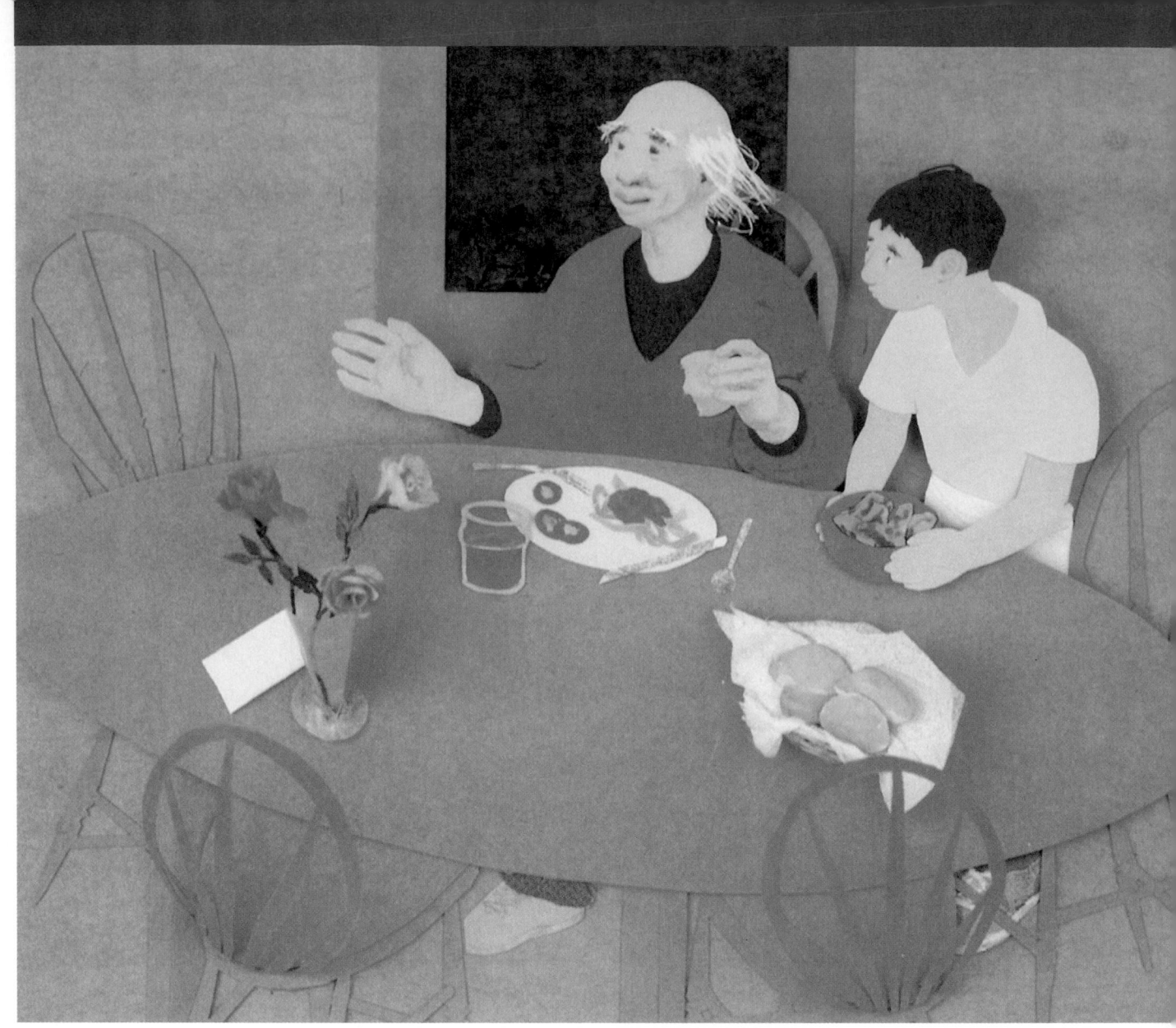

When the stranger had finished, he said to his host, "I cannot pay you with money, but I would like to thank you in my own way."

He picked up a paper napkin from the table and folded it into the shape of a crane. "You have only to clap your hands," he said, "and this bird will come to life and dance for you. Take it, and enjoy it while it is with you."

With these words the stranger left.

It happened just as the stranger had said.
The owner had only to clap his hands and
the paper crane became a living bird, flew
down to the floor, and danced.

146

Soon word of the dancing crane spread,
and people came from far and near to see the
magic bird perform.

The owner was happy again, for his
restaurant was always full of guests.

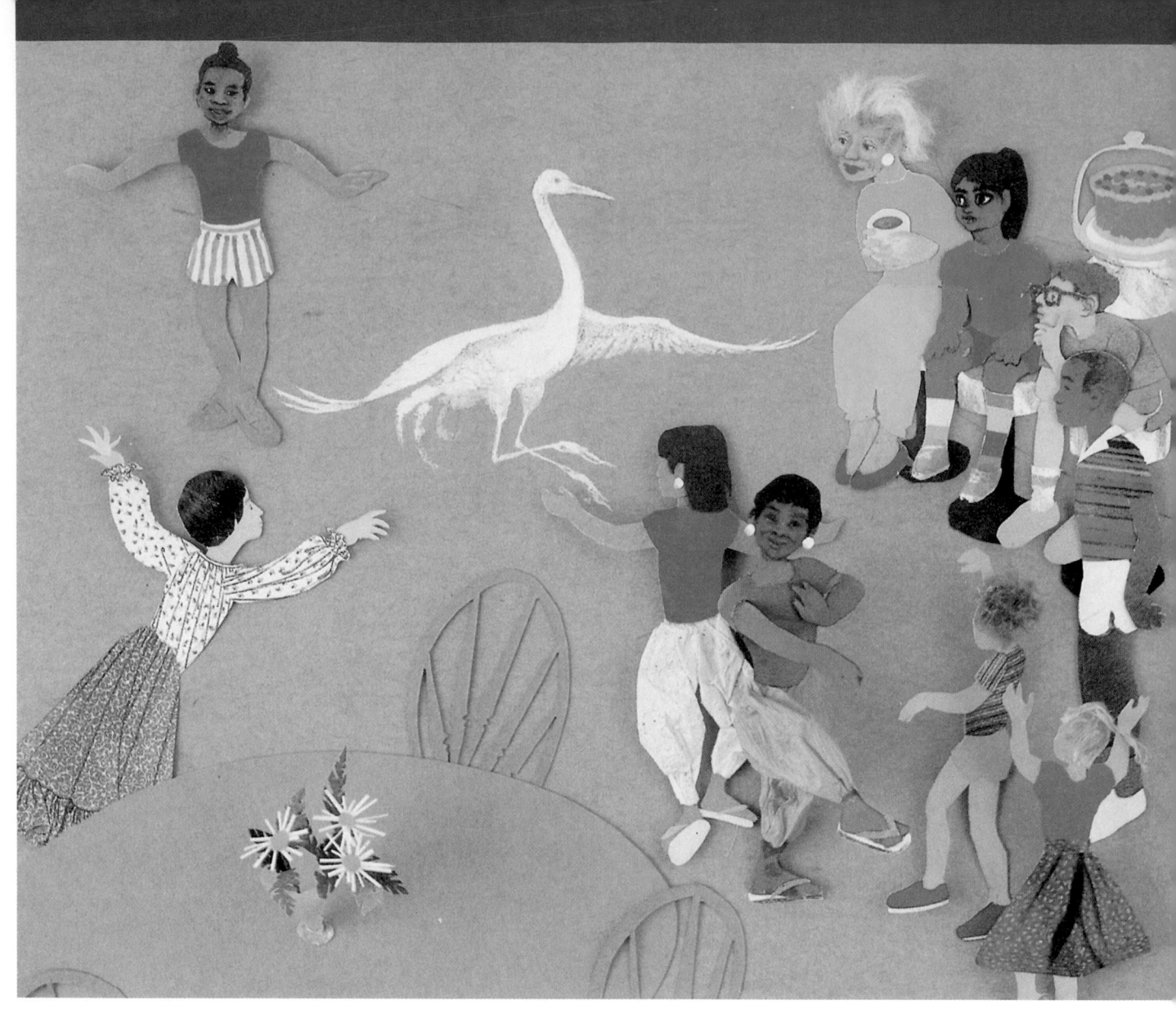

He cooked and served and had company
from morning until night.

The weeks passed.

And the months.

One evening a man came into the
restaurant. His clothes were old and worn,
but he had an unusual, gentle manner. The
owner knew him at once and was overjoyed.

The stranger, however, said nothing. He took a flute from his pocket, raised it to his lips, and began to play.

The crane flew down from its place on the shelf and danced as it had never danced before.

The stranger finished playing, lowered the
flute from his lips, and returned it to his
pocket. He climbed on the back of the crane,
and they flew out of the door and away.

The restaurant still stands by the side of the
road, and guests still come to eat the good
food and hear the story of the gentle stranger
and the magic crane made from a paper
napkin. But neither the stranger nor the
dancing crane has ever been seen again.

The Paper Crane

Concept Connections

Linking the Selection

Writer's Notebook Answer these questions in the Response Journal section of your Writer's Notebook.

- Why do you think the stranger gave the restaurant owner the paper crane?

- How was the paper crane able to help the restaurant owner?

Exploring Concept Vocabulary

The concept word for this lesson is *rewarding.* If you do not know what this word means, look it up in the dictionary. Answer this question:

- Why is showing kindness often a *rewarding* experience?

In the Vocabulary section of your Writer's Notebook, complete the following sentence with a selection vocabulary word.

The kindness of the restaurant owner turned out to be a *rewarding* experience for him and for _____.

Expanding the Concept

Think about "The Paper Crane" and the other unit selections you have read. What have you learned about kindness?

Try to use the word **_rewarding_** as you talk about these stories. Then add new ideas about kindness to the Concept/Question Board.

Meet the Author and Illustrator

Molly Bang's love of books began early. Her parents often gave each other books for birthdays and other holidays. After graduating from Wellesley College, she went to Japan to teach English.

Through her travels in other countries she has gathered many ideas for her books. In her writings she likes to blend Asian folktale themes with modern settings. Her illustrations show a real understanding of the people and places she writes about. She has even illustrated books for her mother, who is also an author.

Focus Questions In what ways can we show kindness to nature? Have you ever had to "let go" of something you love because it was the kind thing to do?

Butterfly House

by Eve Bunting
illustrated by Greg Shed

When I was just a little girl
I saw a small black creature
like a tiny worm,
and saved it from a **greedy** jay
who wanted it
for lunch.

I carried it inside,
safe on its wide green leaf.
My grandpa said
it was a larva
and soon would be
a butterfly.

157

We laid the larva carefully
on thistle leaves
inside an empty jar,
put in a twig
for it to climb—
then made a lid
of soft white paper
all stuck around with glue.
My grandpa knew
exactly what to do.
"I raised a butterfly myself," he said,
"when I was just your age."

How strange to think
my grandpa once
was young like me.
"We would have been best friends
if I'd been there back then," I said.
My grandpa smiled.
"It worked out anyhow.
We're best friends now."

Up in his room
we found a box.
I cut a window in its side,
then covered it with screen.
Soon I could look inside and see
my larva
looking back at me.

What would she see?
A human face
so big and scary,
strange and starey?
What would she think?

"I want it pretty till she goes," I said.
And so
Grandpa and I drew flowers
on colored paper.
Cone flowers, purple-blue,
and marigolds,
lantana, bright as flame,
and thistles, too.

We wedged a garden twig inside the box
for her to walk on,
so her wings could dry
once she became a butterfly.

My grandpa knows
the flowers
butterflies like best.
The ones where they can rest
and drink
the sweet, clear nectar.

We glued the painted flowers inside the box
so it was bright with color.
Made a sky above
the lid all blue
with small white cotton clouds,
and green with tops of trees
that seemed to sway
in soundless air.

"Our Painted Lady," Grandpa said.
"It's time."
　He meant that it was time
　for her to leave
　for her new life.
　I swallowed tears.
　From the beginning I had known
　today would come.
　Now it was here.
　My grandpa took my hand.
"Cry if you like," he said.
"We understand."

We carried out the box and raised the lid.
I watched her falter
as she felt
the first warm touch of sun,
saw trees,
felt breezes brush across her wings.
She rose,
then rested on the fig tree branch.
I saw her fly.

"Good-bye."

My neighbors cannot understand.
"Our flowers are the same as yours,"
  they say each time they visit me.
"We even planted thistles
  to invite the butterflies,
  but they don't come.
They fill your air
  like autumn leaves
  although it isn't fall.
It's such a mystery."

I smile.
It's not a mystery at all.

I think my Painted Ladies
talk among themselves
of how their great-great-grandma,
too far back to say,
was saved
from being eaten by a jay.

"This young girl made a house for her,"
they whisper as they fly.
"A painted garden in a box,
so she'd see beauty
as she hung in that half sleep
that we've all known."

173

174

"This is the girl,
but older now.
We visit her each spring
to give her back
the love she gave to us
so long ago."

It's not a mystery to me.
I think I know.

Butterfly House

Concept Connections

Linking the Selection

 Answer these questions in the Response Journal section of your Writer's Notebook.

- How did the young girl show kindness to the larva?
- How did the grandfather show kindness?

Exploring Concept Vocabulary

The concept word for this lesson is ***consideration.*** If you do not know what this word means, look it up in the dictionary. Answer these questions:

- What does ***consideration*** have to do with kindness?
- How did the young girl show ***consideration*** for the larva while it was developing?

Complete the following sentence with a selection vocabulary word.

Many years later, butterflies still remembered the kindness and ***consideration*** of the woman who long ago _____ .

Expanding the Concept

Think about "Butterfly House" and the other unit selections you have read. What have you learned about kindness?

Try to use the word **consideration** as you talk about the characters and their actions in these stories.

Meet the Author

Eve Bunting grew up in Ireland. Nine years after she got married, she and her family moved to the United States. She believes the world is full of ideas for her stories. *"I couldn't possibly write about all the interesting things I see. There aren't enough hours in the day,"* she said. Bunting has used her ideas to write about horses running free, kings, sharks, whales, and many other things.

Meet the Illustrator

Greg Shed began attending drawing classes right after high school. He was influenced by the impressionists and, with a lot of practice, taught himself how to paint. Shed began illustrating books when his family and friends encouraged him to share his work with publishers. Shed enjoys combining his artistic talents and passion for American history in children's books. He enjoys music, traveling, and ancient cultures.

The Good Samaritan. 1618–1622. **Domenico Fetti.** Oil on wood. 60 × 43.2 cm. The Metropolitan Museum of Art, New York, NY.

General and Horse from the Tomb of Emperor Tang Taizong. 7th century. Stone relief. University of Pennsylvania Museum.

Susan Comforting the Baby. 1881. **Mary Cassatt.** Oil on canvas. The Museum of Fine Arts, Houston.

Corduroy

by Don Freeman

Corduroy is a bear who once lived in the toy department of a big store. Day after day he waited with all the other animals and dolls for someone to come along and take him home.

The store was always filled with shoppers buying all sorts of things, but no one ever seemed to want a small bear in green overalls.

Then one morning a little girl stopped and looked straight into Corduroy's bright eyes.

"Oh, Mommy!" she said. "Look! There's the very bear I've always wanted."

"Not today, dear." Her mother sighed. "I've spent too much already. Besides, he doesn't look new. He's lost the button to one of his shoulder straps."

Corduroy watched them sadly as they walked away.

"I didn't know I'd lost a button," he said to himself. "Tonight I'll go and see if I can find it."

Late that evening, when all the shoppers had gone and the doors were shut and locked, Corduroy climbed carefully down from his shelf and began searching everywhere on the floor for his lost button.

Suddenly he felt the floor moving under him! Quite by accident he had stepped onto an escalator—and up he went!

"Could this be a mountain?" he wondered. "I think I've always wanted to climb a mountain."

He stepped off the escalator as it
reached the next floor, and there, before
his eyes, was a most amazing sight—
tables and chairs and lamps and sofas, and
rows and rows of beds. "This must be a
palace!" Corduroy gasped. "I guess I've
always wanted to live in a palace."

He wandered around admiring the
furniture.

"This must be a bed," he said. "I've
always wanted to sleep in a bed." And up
he crawled onto a large, thick mattress.

All at once he saw something small
and round.

"Why, here's my button!" he cried.
And he tried to pick it up. But, like all the
other buttons on the mattress, it was tied
down tight.

He yanked and pulled with both paws
until POP! Off came the button—and off
the mattress Corduroy toppled, *bang* into a
tall floor lamp. Over it fell with a crash!

Corduroy didn't know it, but there was someone else awake in the store. The night watchman was going his rounds on the floor above. When he heard the crash he came dashing down the escalator.

"Now who in the world did that!" he exclaimed. "Somebody must be hiding around here!"

He flashed his light under and over sofas and beds until he came to the biggest bed of all. And there he saw two fuzzy brown ears sticking up from under the cover.

"Hello!" he said. "How did *you* get upstairs?"

The watchman tucked Corduroy under his arm and carried him down the escalator and set him on the shelf in the toy department with the other animals and dolls.

Corduroy was just waking up when the first customers came into the store in the morning. And there, looking at him with a wide, warm smile, was the same little girl he'd seen only the day before.

"I'm Lisa," she said, "and you're going to be my very own bear. Last night I counted what I've saved in my piggy bank and my mother said I could bring you home."

"Shall I put him in a box for you?" the saleslady asked.

"Oh, no thank you," Lisa answered. And she carried Corduroy home in her arms.

She ran all the way up four flights of stairs, into her family's apartment, and straight to her own room.

Corduroy blinked. There was a chair
and a chest of drawers, and alongside a
girl-size bed stood a little bed just the
right size for him. The room was small,
nothing like that enormous palace in the
department store.

"This must be home," he said. "I *know*
I've always wanted a home!"

Lisa sat down with Corduroy on her lap
and began to sew a button on his overalls.
"I like you the way you are," she said,
"but you'll be more comfortable with your
shoulder strap fastened."

"You must be a friend," said Corduroy.
"I've always wanted a friend."

"Me too!" said Lisa, and gave him a
big hug.

Corduroy

Concept Connections

Linking the Selection

Writer's Notebook Answer these questions in the Response Journal section of your Writer's Notebook.

• How was Lisa kind to Corduroy?

• Who else was kind to Corduroy? What did he do?

Exploring Concept Vocabulary

The concept word for this lesson is *longing.* If you do not know what this word means, look it up in the dictionary. Answer these questions:

• For what did Corduroy have a *longing?*

• For what did Lisa have a *longing?*

Complete the following sentence with a selection vocabulary word.

Lisa's kindness to Corduroy when she first saw him increased his *longing* to leave the _____.

Expanding the Concept

Think about "Corduroy" and the other unit selections you have read. What have you learned about kindness?

Try to use the word **longing** as you talk about these stories. Then add new ideas about kindness to the Concept/Question Board.

Meet the Author and Illustrator

Don Freeman had a job playing the trumpet until he left his trumpet in the subway in New York City. He forgot his trumpet because he was so busy drawing for his art class. From then on, Freeman made his living drawing pictures. Freeman wrote and illustrated his first children's book for his young son, Roy. Many more books followed, including "Corduroy."

Focus Questions Do you give kindness when you might not get it in return? What kind things does your family do for you when you are sick?

April Medicine

Joyce Carol Thomas
illustrated by Floyd Cooper

My mother's touch, so tender, so certain
Steadies me with healing hands
Hands that cool my brow when I perspire
And warm me when I shiver

My mother's hands already know
The temperature of my head
The weather of my heart
How do they know to be cool when I'm hot
And warm when I'm not?

The Story of Three Whales

Giles Whittell
illustrated by Patrick Benson

For twelve bright weeks every summer,
the Arctic Ocean is full of life. Blooms of
plankton float among the icebergs. Shellfish
slide along the sea floor. Squid lurk under
pitch-black overhangs of rock. And whales
swim up from the Pacific to feed.

Humpback whales, Bowhead whales and California Gray whales all come to the Arctic. In the summer of 1988 one particular herd of California Grays was plunging and rolling, leaping and belly-flopping, off the north coast of Alaska.

But winter came early in 1988. The first sign
was a freezing wind from the east. Blizzards
blew in from the top of the world. Thick
pack-ice spread out from the shore and its
shadow fell over the whales.

Most of the whales were quick to sense the changes. In small groups, they set off on the long swim south to warmth for the winter. But three of the whales failed to notice the end of summer—one adult, one middle-sized, one baby.

Quietly the ice crept in. The ocean was
changing from blue to silent white. Gray
whales hold their breath under water for
half an hour, but soon the three who had
been left behind would have nowhere
left to surface.

Only the open water was safe, beyond the pack-ice. But the three whales lost their sense of direction. They swam toward land, into an Alaskan bay, where the still, shallow water was certain to freeze very quickly.

At the mouth of the bay was a shelf of ice, under water. Broken pack-ice piled up against it, forming a wall. From sea-bed to surface there was no way out.

Then the surface froze solid. The whales were trapped in a prison of ice. They could not breathe. Again and again they rammed upward at the ice with their noses.

At last they managed to push their great heads through a crack in the ice. An Inuit hunter was passing and saw them. In nearby Barrow, an Inuit town, he told people what he had seen.

To begin with nothing was done to save the whales. It would be natural for the whales to die and the Inuit accepted it. But the news of the whales began to spread. Their pictures appeared on local TV.

One person who heard the news was
a wildlife ranger. She persuaded the
people of Barrow to help keep the whales
alive. Out over the ice they trudged, with
axes, ice-poles and chainsaws to cut
breathing holes.

The whales appeared at the holes and filled their huge lungs. The Inuit gave them names: Siku (the biggest), Poutu (the middle one) and Kannick (the baby). *Siku* means ice in Inuit. *Poutu* means ice-hole and *Kannick* means snowflake.

The Inuit cut a line of breathing holes,
out toward the open water. They worked
for fourteen days and nights. Clattering
chainsaws sliced constantly through the
ice, but the water would quickly freeze
solid again.

Siku, Poutu and Kannick refused to follow the line of holes. They stayed by the shore where they knew they could breathe. "The Plight of the Whales" became front-page news all over the world. Millions of people waited in hope.

From all across America, offers of help poured in. But nothing could break through the wall of ice at the mouth of the bay. An enormous bulldozer tried, but stuck fast.

A sky-crane helicopter hammered the ice with a concrete torpedo. It punched a line of holes from the whales to the wall. But still the whales wouldn't follow.

Their noses were bloody and scraped to the bone. The ice was invincible. It seemed to the watching world that the whales must die. Polar bears stalked the ice, waiting patiently for a feast of whale-meat.

One evening Siku and Poutu surfaced alone. Being the smallest, Kannick was also the weakest. Morning came and still only Siku and Poutu appeared at the hole. No one could say exactly what had happened. And no one ever saw Kannick again.

On the twentieth day, Siku and Poutu
felt the tremble of distant engines. A huge
Russian ice-breaker was roaring to the
rescue, the great *Admiral Makarov*.

The captain found a grand phrase to mark
the occasion. "Let us begin to break ice!" he
called. All night the breaker charged at the
ice, pulled back, and charged again.

By morning a channel was clear, a quarter of a mile wide. The crew of the *Admiral Makarov* grinned. They came ashore to celebrate and the Inuit and other Americans hugged them and cheered.

Then the ice-breaker turned for the open sea with Siku and Poutu close behind. The whales understood that they must follow the thunder and froth of the engines. The sound would lead them from the prison of ice, to the open water and freedom.

The rest of the herd was three weeks ahead on the journey south. Siku and Poutu had thousands of miles to swim. So they each blew a great waterspout and set off.

Their long ordeal was over now.

The Story of Three Whales

Concept Connections

Linking the Selection

Writer's Notebook Answer these questions in the Response Journal section of your Writer's Notebook.

- Why did the people care about the whales?

- What happened after the first attempts to free the whales failed?

Exploring Concept Vocabulary

The concept word for this lesson is ***determined.*** If you do not know what this word means, look it up in the dictionary. Answer this question:

- Why were the people ***determined*** to help the whales?

In the Vocabulary section of your Writer's Notebook, complete the following sentence with a selection vocabulary word.

The people were ***determined*** to _____.

Expanding the Concept

Think about "The Story of Three Whales" and the other unit selections you have read. What have you learned about kindness?

Try to use the word **determined** as you talk about the characters and their actions in these stories. Then add new ideas about kindness to the Concept/Question Board.

Meet the Author

Giles Whittell grew up in Kenya, Nigeria, and Algeria. In 1989 he rode his bicycle from Berlin to Bulgaria and then wrote about his trip. He is a reporter for a newspaper in Los Angeles.

Meet the Illustrator

Patrick Benson was born and lives in England. He worked in filmmaking and sculpture before he began illustrating books for children. He has illustrated twenty-five children's books. *"What I really want is to get good pictures to as many children as possible."*

Cinderella

retold by Fabio Coen
illustrated by Lane Yerkes

Once there was a girl who was very kind and patient. Her wicked stepmother called her Cinderella because she often sat by the fireplace close to the cinders.

222

Her stepmother made her work all day long. She had to light the fire, prepare the meals, wash the dishes, clean the house, and make beautiful gowns for her two stepsisters, who were very ugly and very mean.

Cinderella was always dressed in rags, but she was more beautiful in her rags than her stepsisters in their beautiful gowns.

One day the King and Queen gave a ball.
Cinderella helped her stepmother and her
stepsisters to get ready. Then the three of them
went to the ball.

Cinderella was all alone. She began to cry.
Suddenly her Fairy Godmother appeared. "Why
are you crying?" she asked Cinderella.

"I, too, would have liked to go to the ball,"
Cinderella replied.

"Then you shall go," said her Fairy Godmother. "Bring me a pumpkin from the garden."

With one touch of her magic wand, Cinderella's Fairy Godmother turned the pumpkin into a beautiful carriage. Then she took six mice from a trap. A touch of the magic wand turned them into six prancing horses. In the cellar Cinderella's Fairy Godmother found a large rat. She turned him into a large coachman with a great mustache.

227

Another touch of the magic wand and Cinderella's rags turned into a beautiful silver gown covered with diamonds. On her feet were a pair of little glass slippers.

As she stepped into the carriage, her Fairy Godmother said, "Have a good time, but remember this. You must leave the ball before midnight. When the clock strikes twelve, your carriage will turn into a pumpkin, your horses into mice, your coachman into a rat, and your gown into rags."

Cinderella promised to leave the ball before midnight. Then they drove away.

Cinderella was so beautiful that the prince danced with her all night. She forgot about her Fairy Godmother's warning. The clock began to strike twelve. Cinderella ran out of the palace and down the stairs. In her hurry she lost one of her glass slippers.

The prince ran after Cinderella, but it was too late. By the time he reached the bottom of the stairs, her beautiful carriage was gone. The prince found only her little glass slipper.

The prince had fallen in love with Cinderella. He wanted to find her, but he didn't even know her name or where she lived. He sent a page to every house in the kingdom. In each house the page asked every girl to try on the slipper. But their feet were much too big for the tiny slipper.

At last the page came to the house where Cinderella lived. Her two stepsisters hurried to try on the little slipper. But their feet were much too big. No matter how hard they tried, they could not get the slipper on.

Then it was Cinderella's turn. The slipper fit her perfectly. At that moment her Fairy Godmother appeared and dressed Cinderella in a gown of shimmering gold.

Cinderella and the prince were married. Because she was so kind, Cinderella forgave her wicked stepmother and stepsisters, and they all lived happily ever after.

Cinderella

Concept Connections

Linking the Selection

Writer's Notebook Answer these questions in the Response Journal section of your Writer's Notebook.

- How was kindness shown to Cinderella?

- How did Cinderella show kindness?

Exploring Concept Vocabulary

The concept word for this lesson is *forgive.* If you do not know what this word means, look it up in the dictionary. Answer these questions:

- In the story, whom did Cinderella *forgive?*

- Why did Cinderella *forgive* her stepmother and stepsisters?

In the Vocabulary section of your Writer's Notebook, write a sentence using the word *forgive* and one of the selection vocabulary words.

Expanding the Concept

Think about "Cinderella" and the other unit selections. What have you learned about kindness?

Try to use the word *forgive* as you talk about these stories. Then add new ideas to the Concept/Question Board.

Meet the Author

Fabio Coen was born in Rome, Italy. He came to the United States in 1940 and later became a citizen. He loved books and went to work for a publishing company. While he worked there he helped other authors of children's books get started.

Meet the Illustrator

Lane Yerkes has created illustrations for advertising, newspapers, magazines, textbooks, and logos. He has written and illustrated two children's stories that he hopes to publish. His home is located on the southwest coast of Florida, just above the Everglades. He lives with his wife and their dog. When not working, he enjoys boating and fishing.

Look Again

Seeing is believing. Or is it? Can you always trust what you see? Can something look like one thing and really be something different? Maybe!

Focus Questions Why do animals need to hide? What does "there's more to the animal world than meets the eye" mean?

I See Animals Hiding

by Jim Arnosky

I see animals hiding. I see a porcupine high in a tree.

Wild animals are shy and always hiding. It is natural for them to be this way. There are many dangers in the wild.

Even when they are caught unaware out in the open, wild animals try to hide. They stay behind whatever is available—a thin tree trunk or even a single blade of grass. Most of the time they go unnoticed.

The colors of wild animals match the colors of the places where the animals live. Because of this protective coloration, called camouflage, wild animals can hide by simply staying still and blending in.

Woodcocks and other birds, which spend much of their time on the woodland floor, have patterns and colors like those of dry leaves.

I see animals hiding. I see two woodcocks on the leafy ground.

Of all wild animals, deer are the wariest. Even though their colors are camouflaged, they feel safe only where there are good hiding places nearby.

In a summer meadow of tall grasses and small shrubby trees, deer can hide quickly by just lying down.

There are 20 deer on the snowy hill.
Can you find them all?

In autumn, deer shed their red-brown summer coats and replace them with warmer, grayer winter coats that better match the gray and brown trunks of leafless trees.

I see animals hiding. I see a whole herd of deer on a winter hill.

Snowshoe hares change from summer brown to winter white. The only way to spot a snowshoe hare in a snowy scene is to look for its shiny black eyes.

Squint your eyes and you will see just how invisible a snowshoe hare on snow can be.

Here are three more animals that are as white as snow. The arctic fox and long-tailed weasel change from winter white to summer brown. The snowy owl stays white year-round.

The colors and patterns of screech owls blend perfectly with tree bark. These small owls can sleep all day out in the open and not be discovered.

Besides an owl, there is one other bark imitator on this tree. Can you tell what it is?

I see animals hiding. I see an owl and a moth on a limb.

Trout are camouflaged by color and shape to blend with the smooth mossy stones in a stream.

Looking down in a brook, I see a speckled trout swimming amid speckled stones.

I see animals hiding. I see a garter snake slithering through the grass.

Up close a snake in the grass may be easy to see. But as long as the snake keeps a safe distance from its enemies, it can sneak by, looking like just another broken branch on the ground.

Stand back a few steps from this page, and using only your eyes, try to follow the line of the snake from its head to its tail. Can you tell what is snake and what is stick?

A bittern is a wading bird whose brown streaks and long sticklike legs naturally blend in with the cattails and reeds that grow along shorelines.

When a bittern really needs to be invisible, it points its bill upward and sways its long neck, like a cattail swaying gently in a breeze.

And last but not least:
Animals hide by staying inside.

I See Animals Hiding

Concept Connections

Linking the Selection

Answer these questions in the Response Journal section of your Writer's Notebook.

- Why is it sometimes difficult to spot animals?

- Why do animals need to hide?

Exploring Concept Vocabulary

The concept word for this lesson is **protection.** If you do not know what this word means, look it up in the dictionary. Answer this question:

- How does an animal's color provide **protection** for it?

Complete the following sentence with a selection vocabulary word.

Camouflage gives animals **protection** and makes them almost _____.

Expanding the Concept

Think about the selection "I See Animals Hiding." What did you learn about animal camouflage?

Try to use the word **protection** as you talk about this selection. Then add new ideas to the Concept/Question Board.

Meet the Author and Illustrator

James Edward Arnosky and his family live in the northern Vermont wilderness. He observes nature while fishing, drawing, or walking. His illustrations try to teach readers how to see as an artist would.

"I write about the world I live in and try to share all I see and feel in my books." Arnosky often describes the natural world in a way that the reader becomes a part of the scene. He sums up the role of an author saying, *"The best nonfiction lets the reader knock on the door, and you let them in. Then you go away."*

They Thought They Saw Him

Craig Kee Strete

illustrated by José Aruego and Ariane Dewey

• •

Little dark chameleon crept out of the heart of his winter home and moved up onto a tiny branch.

Rain puddles glistened beneath his feet. The wind blew warm over the walls of the adobe. All winter little dark chameleon had lived, safe and asleep, beneath the granary where the people kept their seed corn.

Now insects buzzed over bush and tree, and he was awake.

As he moved on quick, silent feet, he began to forget the sleepy winter dark and felt now the joy in the first wakeful light of spring.

Eyes half closed, still filled with winter memories, little dark chameleon sat on a brown branch and waited for an insect to find his tongue.

A hungry snake watched him. The snake climbed the tree to catch the dark chameleon for his first meal of the spring.

But when he got there, everything on the brown branch was brown.

"The dark chameleon got away," said the snake, and he slithered off.

255

Little brown chameleon jumped off the
brown branch. His feet gripped green leaves,
and he hung there. His sticky tongue caught
a bug.

An owl, flying home to sleep, saw the brown chameleon in the green leaves. The owl swooped down to catch him.

But when he got there, everything in the green leaves was green.

"The brown chameleon got away," hooted the owl, and he flew off.

Little green chameleon jumped out of the green leaves and landed softly in the tan, rain-washed sand.

A fox saw the green chameleon in the sand. With pointed ears and hungry eyes, the fox crept toward him.

But little chameleon had his secret.

"Nobody sees me," he said, "because I am the color of the world."

They Thought They Saw Him

Concept Connections

Linking the Selection

 Writer's Notebook Answer these questions in the Response Journal section of your Writer's Notebook.

- Why did the snake, owl, fox, and boy all think the chameleon got away?

- What was the chameleon's secret?

Exploring Concept Vocabulary

The concept word for this lesson is ***predator.*** If you do not know what this word means, look it up in the dictionary. Answer these questions:

- How does an animal's camouflage protect it from its ***predators?***

- In the story what were the chameleon's ***predators?***

In the Vocabulary section of your Writer's Notebook, write a sentence using the word ***predator*** and one of the selection vocabulary words.

Expanding the Concept

Think about "I See Animals Hiding" and "They Thought They Saw Him." What did you learn about animal camouflage from these selections?

Try to use the word ***predator*** as you talk about these selections. Then add new ideas to the Concept/Question Board.

Meet the Author

Craig Kee Strete writes fiction for children and adults. He also writes for theater, television, and film. Strete's writing often describes the lives of young Native Americans growing up between two cultures. He shows the culture of the Native Americans and their love of nature. "They Thought They Saw Him" is a story that introduces Strete's world to others.

Meet the Illustrators

José Aruego and Ariane Dewey have combined their talents and have illustrated more than sixty children's books. Mr. Aruego does the drawings and Ms. Dewey adds the color through paint.

José Aruego began a career in law, but after a few months he realized that he wanted to draw, not practice law. After graduating from art school, he began drawing cartoons and later began illustrating children's books.

Ariane Dewey always loved bright colors. In fourth grade art class, she painted bright pink kids swimming in a blue-green lake. Her love of joyful colors is seen in many children's books.

The Chameleon

John Gardner
illustrated by Susan Nethery

People say the Chameleon can take on
the hue
Of whatever he happens to be on.
It's true
—Within reason, of course. If you put him on
plaid
Or polka dots, he really gets mad.

266

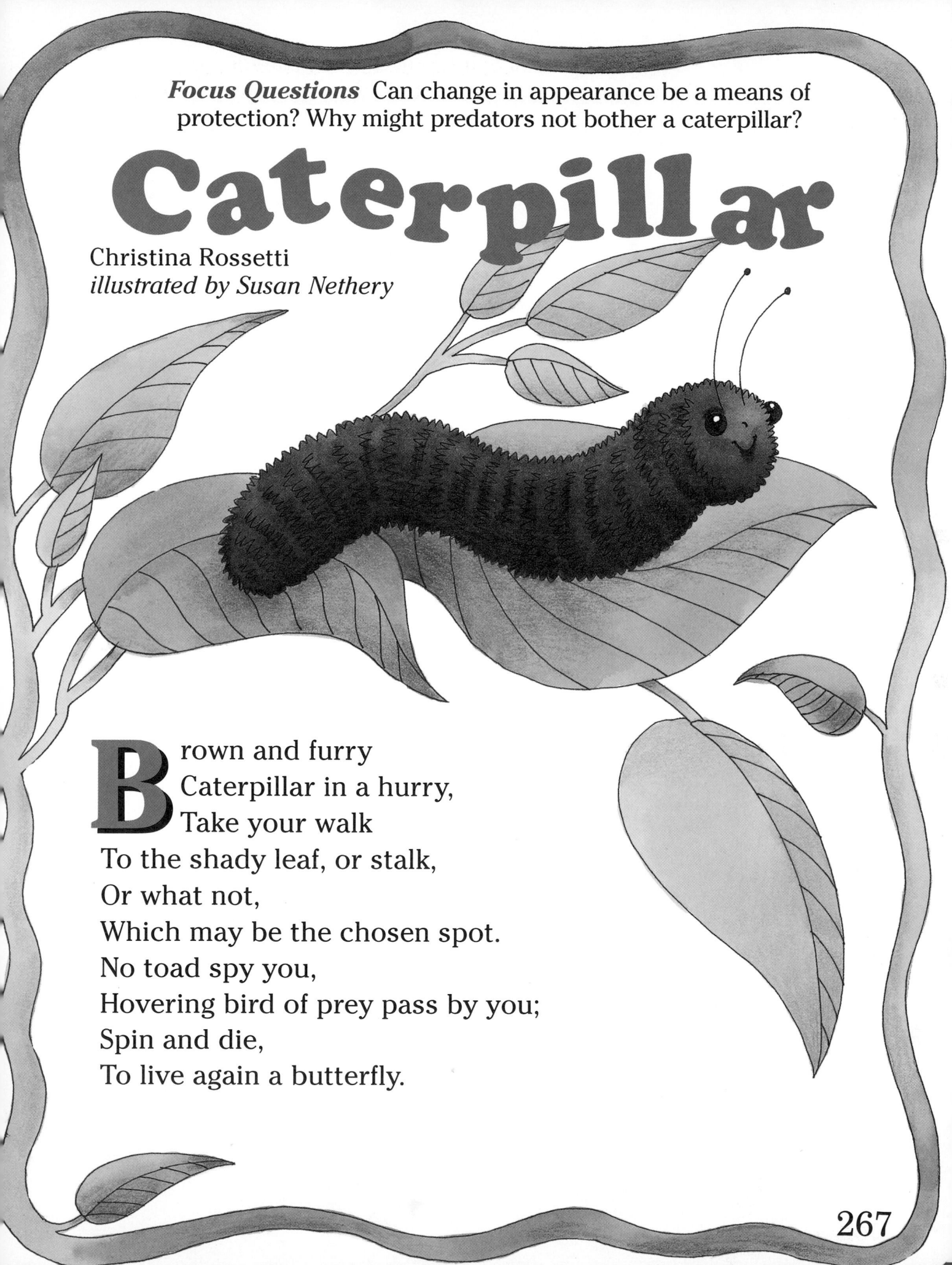

Caterpillar

Christina Rossetti
illustrated by Susan Nethery

Brown and furry
Caterpillar in a hurry,
Take your walk
To the shady leaf, or stalk,
Or what not,
Which may be the chosen spot.
No toad spy you,
Hovering bird of prey pass by you;
Spin and die,
To live again a butterfly.

267

Focus Questions Can animals ever be in danger because they are camouflaged? Have you ever accidentally stepped on an animal or creature? Why did that happen?

HUNGRY LITTLE HARE

by Howard Goldsmith
illustrated by Denny Bond

Little Hare the jackrabbit had great long ears with little black tips. Her long furry hind paws helped her hop very fast and jump very high.

268

One beautiful day, Little Hare smelled raspberries. Raspberry leaves were her favorite food.

Little Hare hopped, and then she hopped
again. She followed the scent of raspberry to
a pond in the meadow.

"Ouch!" a voice cried. "You stepped on me!"
Little Hare looked, but she saw only bright
green grass.

"I can't see you," Little Hare said.

"You're not supposed to see me," said a
green frog, hopping in front of Little Hare.
"My color hides me in the grass from
snoopy snakes. *You* don't eat frogs, do
you?"

"Oh, no!" said Little Hare. "I'm looking for raspberry leaves."

Little Hare hopped, and then she hopped again. *Crunch, crunch, crunch* went the twigs in the woods.

"Ouch!" a voice cried. "You pushed me!"

Little Hare looked, but she saw only brown twigs on a tree stump.

"I can't see you," Little Hare said.

"You're not supposed to see me," said a walkingstick, crawling up to Little Hare. "I look exactly like a twig. That's how I hide from sneaky squirrels."

Little Hare was hungry. She hopped, and then she hopped again, past a big green bush.

"Ouch!" a voice said. "You bumped me!"

Little Hare looked, but she saw only slender green leaves.

"I can't see you," Little Hare said.

"You're not supposed to see me!" A katydid hopped up right in front of Little Hare. "I look exactly like a leaf, but I'm really an insect. My disguise protects me from prying praying mantises."

277

Now Little Hare was *very* hungry. She hopped, and then hopped again, and leaned against a tree to rest.

"Ouch!" said a voice. "Don't lean on me!"

Little Hare looked and looked, but she saw
only brown bark on the tree.

"I can't see you," said Little Hare. "I guess
you look like something else, too."

"That's right," said a moth, fluttering in front
of Little Hare. "My color matches the bark
of a tree, so when I rest the wily
woodpeckers can't find me."

Little Hare was just about to hop off when a drowsy voice exclaimed, "Careful! I'm resting in the leaves at your feet!"

"It means you disappear into the world around you," explained her mother.

"I wish I were invisible like the other animals and insects," said Little Hare.

"You will be," replied her mother. "You only have to wait."

And Mother Hare was right!

HUNGRY LITTLE HARE

Concept Connections

Linking the Selection

Writer's Notebook Answer these questions in the Response Journal section of your Writer's Notebook.

- Why wasn't Little Hare able to see the other animals and insects?

- How was Little Hare able to become invisible?

Exploring Concept Vocabulary

The concept word for this lesson is **surroundings.** If you do not know what this word means, look it up in the dictionary. Answer these questions:

- How do **surroundings** help keep animals from being seen?

- How might an animal's **surroundings** change during the year?

In the Vocabulary section of your Writer's Notebook, write and complete the following sentence using one of the selection vocabulary words.

An animal's **surroundings** and protective coloring provide it with _____.

Expanding the Concept

Think about "Hungry Little Hare" and the other unit selections you have read. What have you learned about animal camouflage?

Try to use the word **surroundings** as you talk about the information in these selections. Then add new ideas about animal camouflage to the Concept/Question Board.

Meet the Author

Howard Goldsmith was a psychologist before he was a children's author. He likes to make his books fun and challenging for his readers. His book, *2000 A.D.* is an adventure story. This is a good story for children who like to watch television space shows and movies. Grown-ups enjoy reading Goldsmith's books too.

Meet the Illustrator

Denny Bond has been an illustrator for many years. In addition to children's books, he has done illustrations for magazines, advertisements, and businesses. He is also a painter and has shown his paintings in art shows and at galleries. He tells young artists, *"dream with your eyes open…and always carry paper and pencil for doodling, or at least to write down ideas that may pop into your head…"*

Exotic Landscape. 1910. **Henri Rousseau.** Oil on canvas.
Norton Simon Foundation, Pasadena, California.

Printed Fabric from Bambalulu Handcraft Center. 1993. **Artist unknown.** Cotton with gold fabric ink. $2 \times 2 \frac{1}{2}$ feet. Private Collection.

Deidre. 1982. **Wendy Fay Dixon.** Silverpoint on paper. $17 \frac{3}{4} \times 17$ in. The National Museum of Women in the Arts, Washington, D.C.

Focus Questions Are land animals the only creatures that use camouflage? If you were a sea creature, how would you hide from your enemies?

How to Hide an Octopus

& other sea creatures

by Ruth Heller

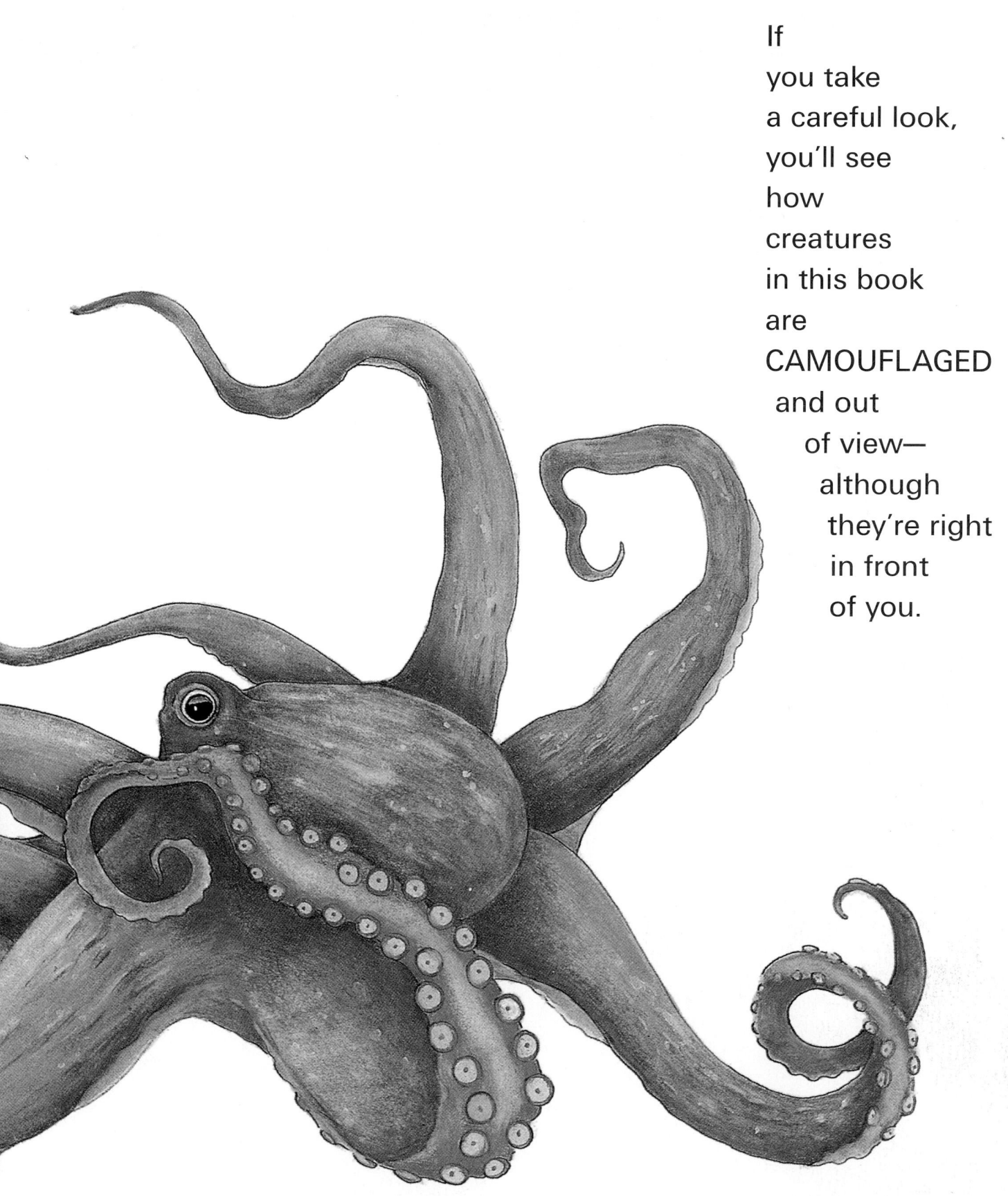

If
you take
a careful look,
you'll see
how
creatures
in this book
are
CAMOUFLAGED
and out
of view—
although
they're right
in front
of you.

As quick as a wink,
it turns to pink
or green or blue
or any hue,
and, if you think
that's not enough,
its skin can
turn
from
smooth to
rough.

This
creature
is an
OCTOPUS
and very often
hides

298

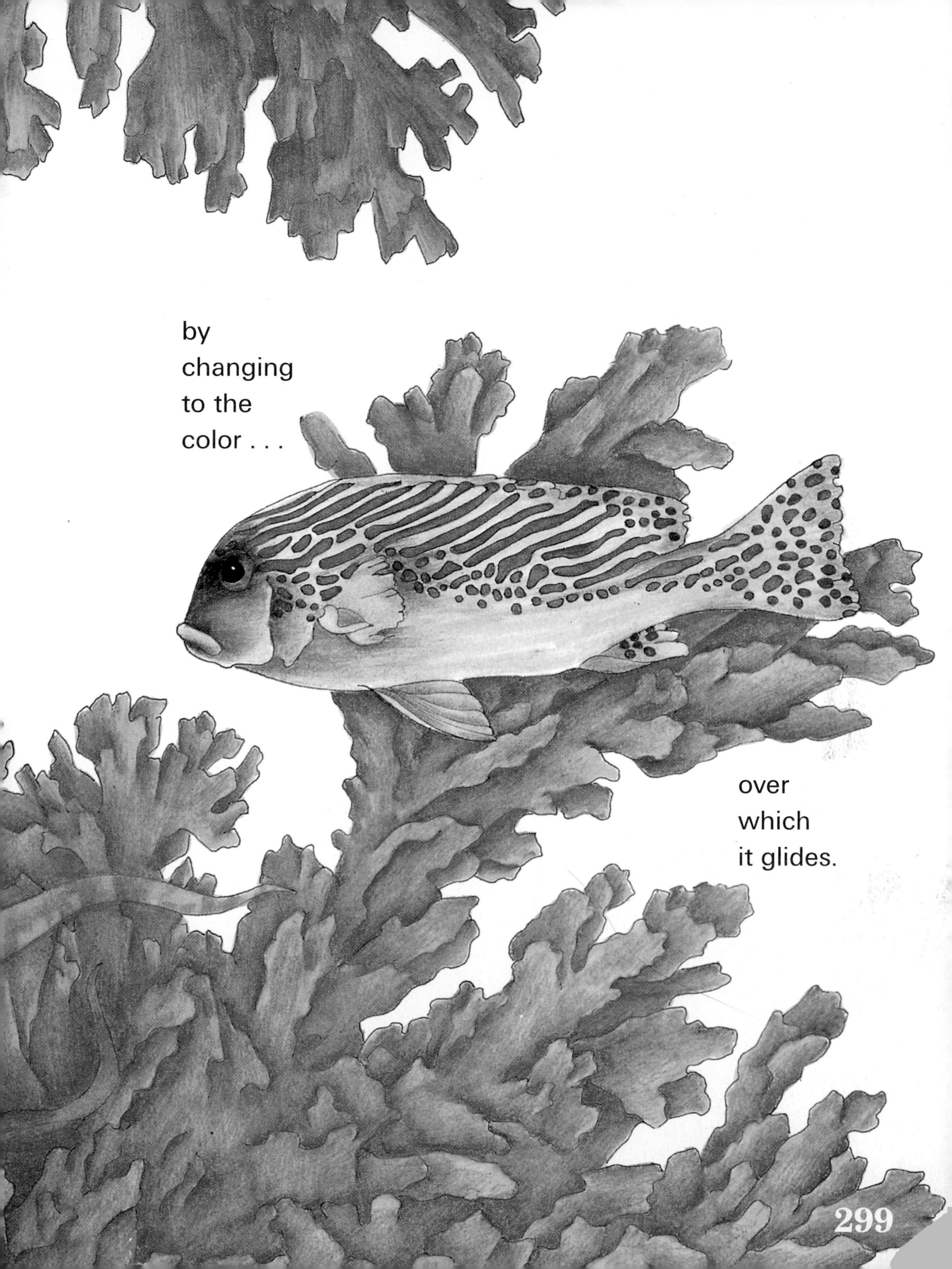

by
changing
to the
color . . .

over
which
it glides.

Its relative,
the
CUTTLEFISH,
could do the same
if he should wish.

The stripes that he is
sporting
show
that he's
been courting,
but
he can
make them
fade away . . .

slowly
or
without
delay.

The
SARGASSUM FISH,
grotesque
at
best,
looks
just
like . . .

302

its seaweed nest.

The
giant red
SEA DRAGON
is
the most bizarre
of all the
creatures
seen so far,
with
ribbons of skin
that grow
from its chin
and
from its
belly and back.

304

They
spread
from its head
and trail from its tail,
and it's
easy to see
why its enemies fail
to find
where it feeds . . .

among the red weeds.

305

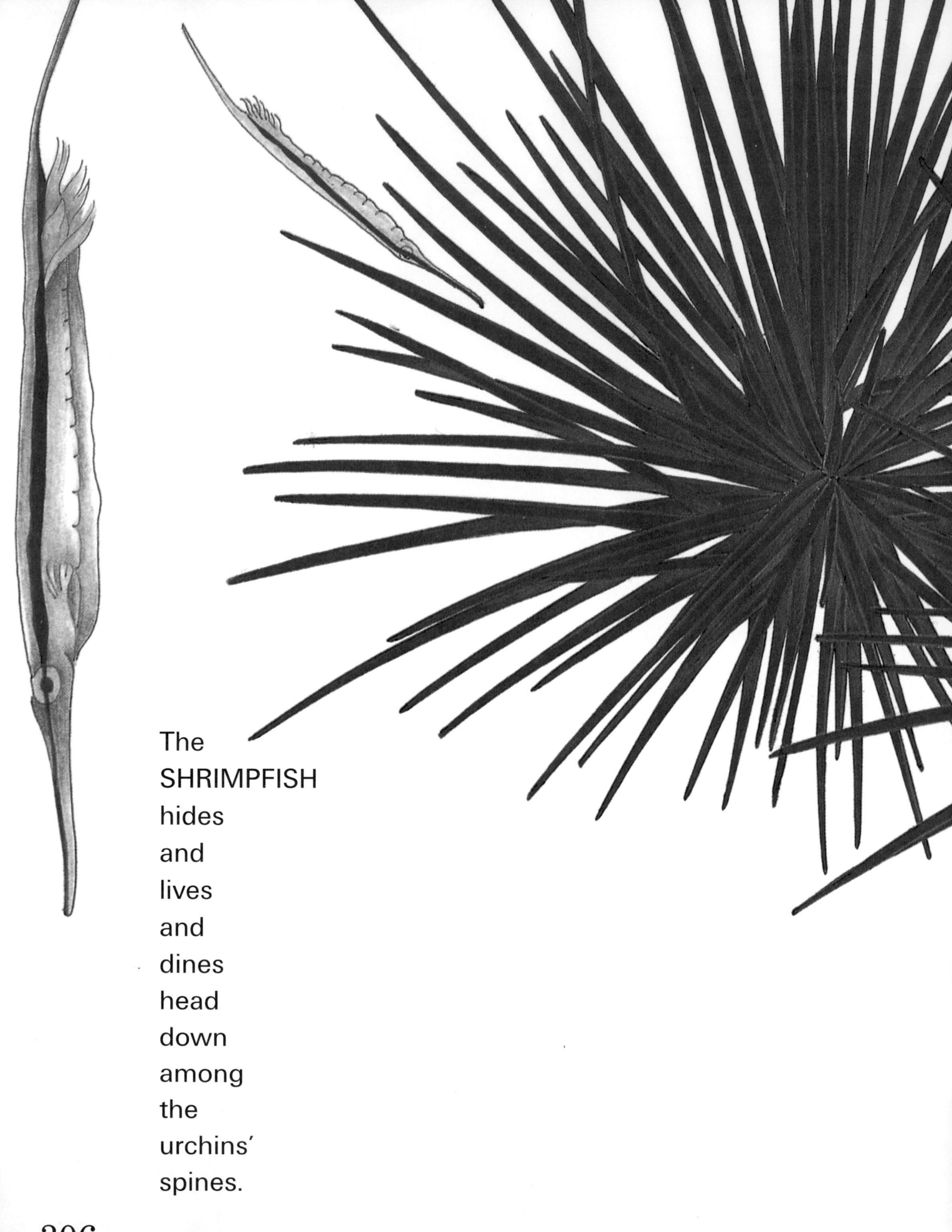

The
SHRIMPFISH
hides
and
lives
and
dines
head
down
among
the
urchins'
spines.

306

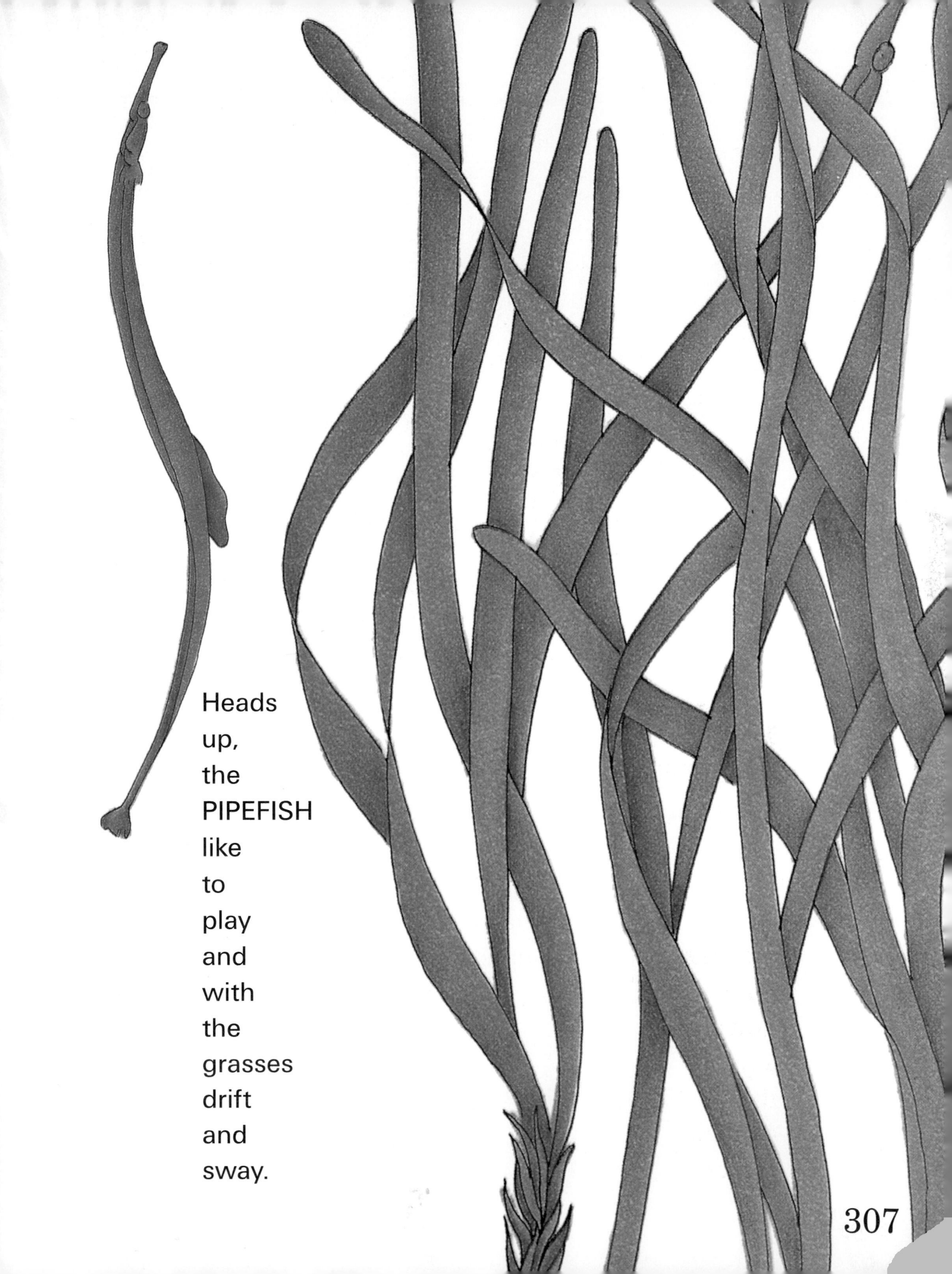

Heads
up,
the
PIPEFISH
like
to
play
and
with
the
grasses
drift
and
sway.

307

The
BUTTERFLY
FISH

has been
designed

to
make
it
very
hard . . .

to
find.

The
DECORATOR CRAB
is drab
and
will not rest
until it's dressed,

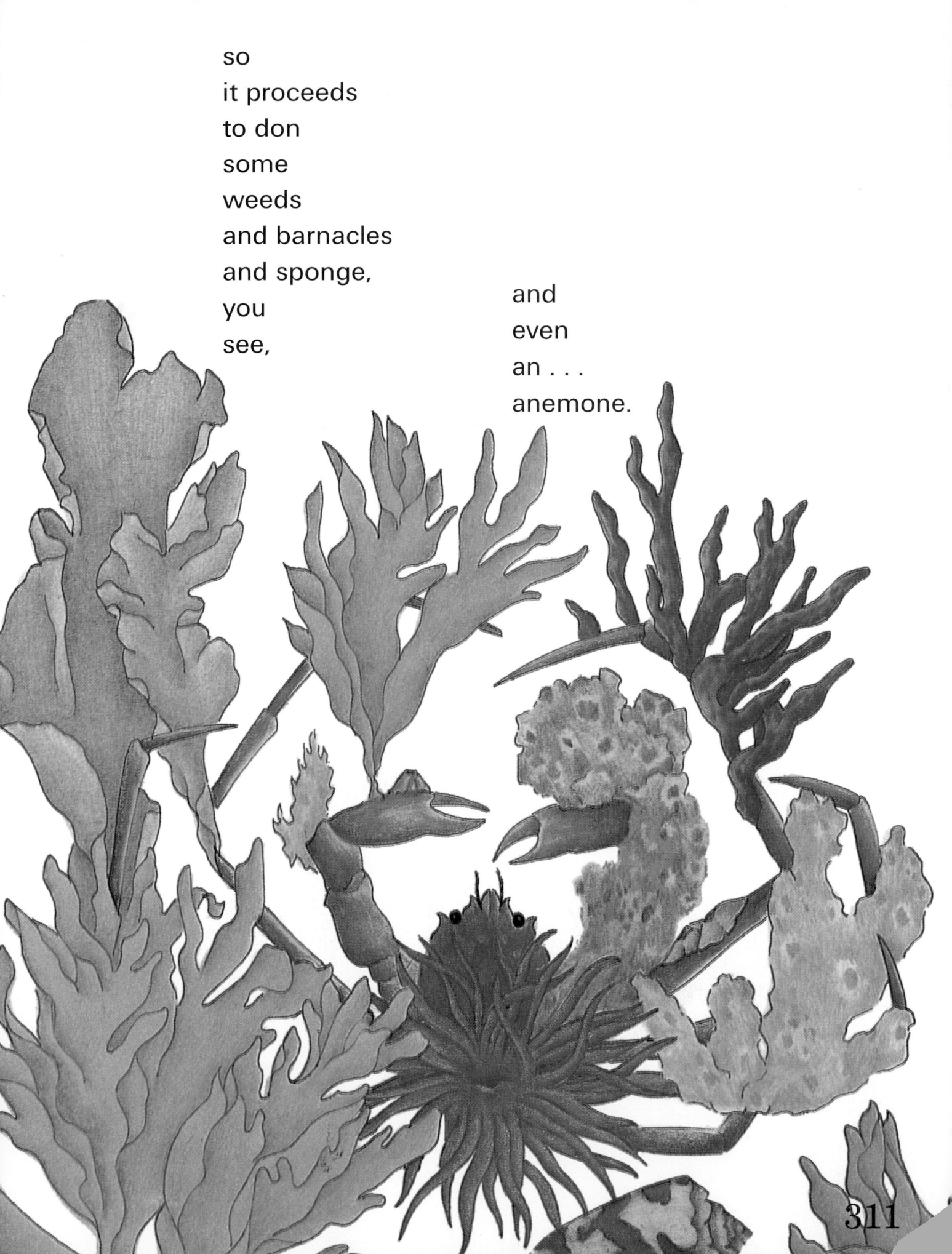

so
it proceeds
to don
some
weeds
and barnacles
and sponge,
you
see,

and
even
an . . .
anemone.

311

How to Hide an Octopus
& other sea creatures

Concept Connections

Linking the Selection

Writer's Notebook Answer these questions in the Response Journal section of your Writer's Notebook.

• How does an octopus hide?

• Why are the sea creatures in this story camouflaged?

Exploring Concept Vocabulary

The concept word for this lesson is ***environment.*** If you do not know what this word means, look it up in the dictionary. Answer these questions:

• How does an animal's ***environment*** help it hide?

• Name some things in a sea creature's ***environment*** that help it hide.

Complete the following sentence with a selection vocabulary word.

An animal's ***environment*** might help to keep it safe from _____.

Expanding the Concept

Think about "How to Hide an Octopus and Other Sea Creatures" and the other unit selections you have read. What have you learned about animal camouflage?

Try to use the word *environment* as you talk about these selections. Then add new ideas to the Concept/Question Board.

Meet the Author

Ruth Heller is a writer and an illustrator. She began her career designing wrapping paper, napkins, kites, mugs, and greeting cards. She even designed coloring books. Once when she was studying tropical fish for a coloring book that she was making, Ruth Heller saw a strange looking shape floating in the fish tank. It was an egg sac. Heller began to read about egg-laying animals. She thought about the egg in the fish tank. Colorful shapes and words began to go through her mind. That was when Ruth Heller decided to write and illustrate children's books. Her first book was called *Chickens Aren't the Only Ones*.

How the Guinea Fowl Got Her Spots

retold and illustrated by Barbara Knutson

A long time ago, when everything had just been made, Nganga the Guinea Fowl had glossy black feathers all over. She had no white speckles as she does today—not a single spot.

314

Guinea Fowl was a little bird, but she had a big friend. And that was Cow.

They liked to go to the great green hills where Cow could eat grass and Nganga could scratch for seeds and crunch grasshoppers.

And they would both keep an eye out for Lion.

One day, Guinea Fowl was crossing the river to meet Cow on the most delicious hill they knew. The grass was so juicy and thick that, even from the river, Nganga could hear Cow hungrily tearing up one mouthful after another.

But . . . what was that Nganga saw slinking toward Cow?

Was it . . . ?

Yes, it was LION!

Now you might think a guinea fowl is no match for a lion, but Nganga didn't think that. In fact, she didn't think at all.

She scratched and scrambled up the bank as fast as she could and whirred right between Cow and Lion, kicking and flapping in the dust.

"RAAUGH!" shouted Lion.

"My eyes! This sand! What was that?"

When the clouds of dust thinned there was no sign of anyone—certainly not any dinner for Lion. He went home in a terrible temper, growling like his empty belly.

The next day, Guinea Fowl was at the grassy patch first. You can be sure she had her eyes wide open for Lion.

Soon she saw Cow cautiously crossing the river to join her—shlip, clop, shlop. But something yellow was twitching in the reeds.

Wasn't that Lion's tail?

Up whirred Nganga, half tumbling, half flying with her stubby wings. Lion looked up, startled, from his hiding place. Frrrr . . . a little black whirlwind was racing across the grass toward the river. "Whe-klo-klo-klo!" it called out to Cow.

"Guinea Fowl! That's where the duststorm came from yesterday," growled Lion between his sharp teeth. But the next moment, the whirlwind hit the river.

"RAAUghmf!" Lion exploded with a roar that ended underwater.

"I'll teach that bird to chase away my dinner!" he spluttered. But by the time his roar was working properly again, Cow and Guinea Fowl were safely over the next hill at Cow's house.

"Nganga," mooed Cow gratefully, "twice you have helped me escape from Lion. Now I will help you do the same."

Turning around, she dipped her tasseled tail into a calabash of milk. Then she shook the tasselful of milk over Guinea Fowl's sleek black feathers—flick, flock, flick—spattering her with creamy white milk.

Guinea Fowl craned her head and admired the delicate speckles covering her back.

She spread her wings, and Cow sprinkled them with milk too—flick, flock, flick.

"Whe-klo-klo! That's beautiful, Cow!" chuckled Nganga. "Thank you, my friend!"

And she set off for home.

Whom should she meet where the path crossed the river but Lion, still shaking the water out of his ears and angrier than ever.

"Ho, Speckled Bird!" snorted Lion. "Have you seen Guinea Fowl on your path?"

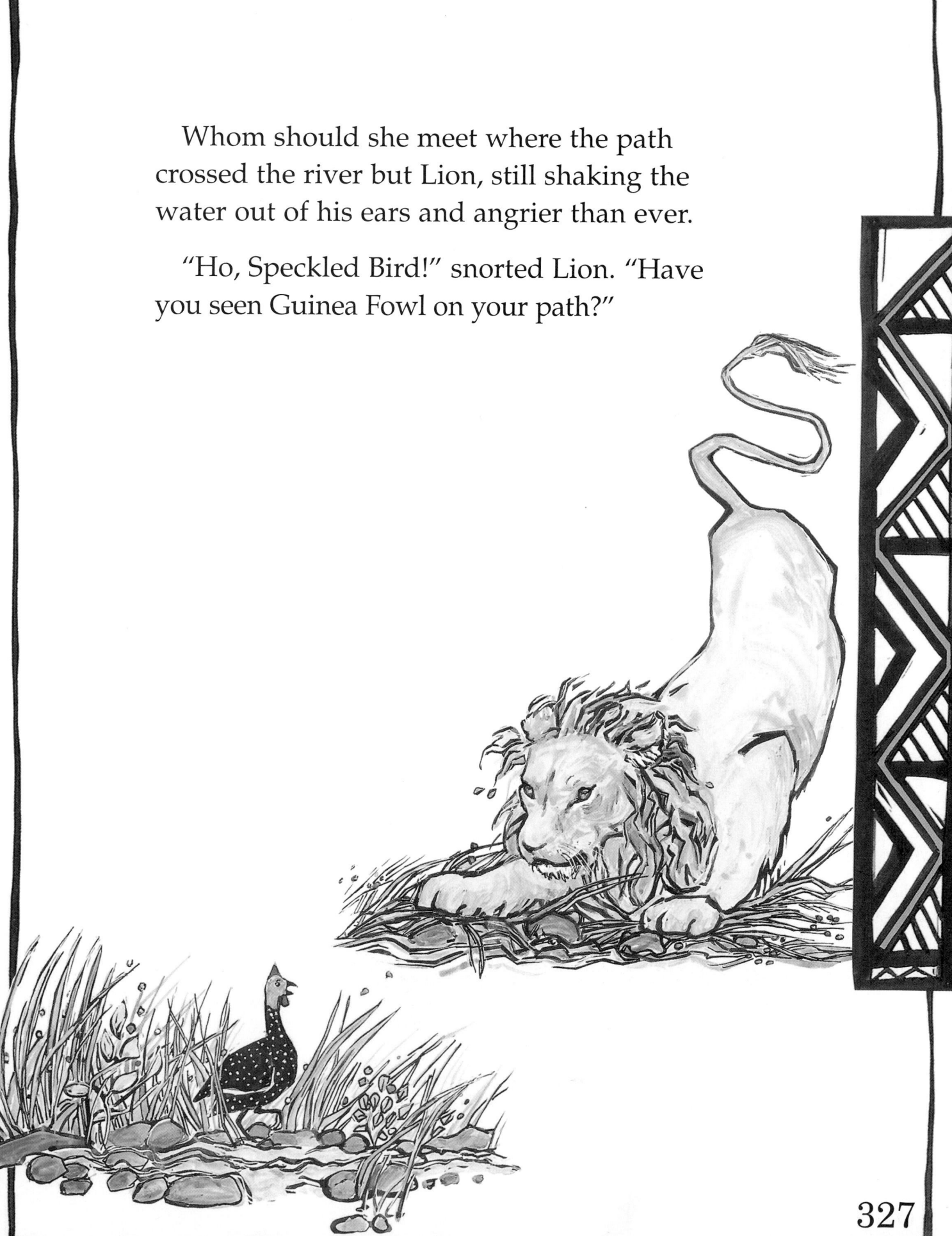

"Oh yes," clucked Nganga, hiding a smile. "I believe she went that way."

She pointed with her spotted wing to the hills far down the river.

"If you go quickly and don't stop to rest, you may catch up with her in a few days."

Lion leaped up at once, not bothering to thank the strange bird. A minute later, he thought about taking her along for a traveling snack, but when he looked back at the riverbank, he could see no trace of her.

"These lovely spots are just the thing for hiding in the shadows and grass!" laughed Nganga, who was, in fact, right where Lion had left her.

And she turned back to Cow's house to thank her friend again.

How the Guinea Fowl Got Her Spots

Concept Connections

Linking the Selection

Writer's Notebook Answer these questions in the Response Journal section of your Writer's Notebook.

- How did Guinea Fowl protect her friend Cow from Lion?

- How did Cow help protect Guinea Fowl?

Exploring Concept Vocabulary

The concept word for this lesson is *survive.* If you do not know what this word means, look it up in the dictionary. Answer these questions:

- How does an animal's camouflage help it *survive?*

- Why did Guinea Fowl and Cow help each other *survive?*

Complete the following sentence with a selection vocabulary word.

Cow helped Guinea Fowl *survive* by spattering white milk on her _____.

332

Expanding the Concept

Think about "How the Guinea Fowl Got Her Spots" and the other unit selections you have read. What have you learned about animal camouflage?

Try to use the word *survive* as you talk about the characters and information in these selections. Then add new ideas about animal camouflage to the Concept/Question Board.

Meet the Author and Illustrator

Barbara Knutson was born in South Africa. She studied art in Africa and the United States. After receiving a degree in art education and French, she taught English and French in an international school in Nigeria.

Having grown up in South Africa and having traveled in other African countries, Barbara Knutson has a lot of personal experiences to use in her illustrations. Her detailed watercolors show the love and knowledge she has of African culture. She now lives in Minnesota where she visits schools and works at a children's bookstore.

Animal Camouflage

by Janet McDonnell

What Is Camouflage?

Have you ever played hide and seek outside? Sometimes it is hard to find a good place to hide! But what if you could paint yourself brown and green like the ground?

Or put on a costume that made you look like a tree? Or lie down and cover yourself with leaves? All of these tricks would make you much harder to find.

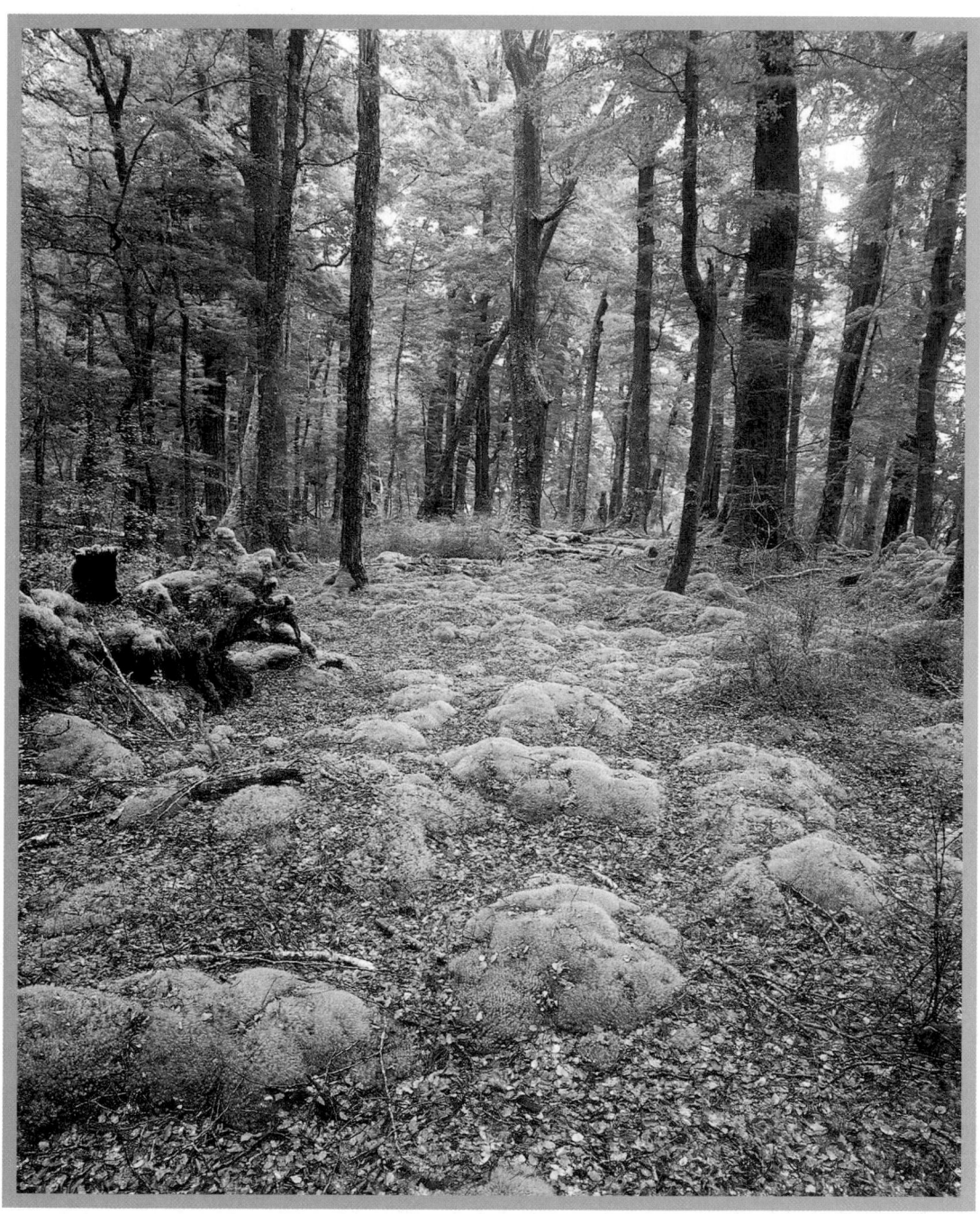

A forest looks green and brown.

What Is Camouflage?

Some animals use tricks to hide themselves. Using colors and patterns to hide is called camouflage. Camouflage makes things very hard to find—even when they are out in the open.

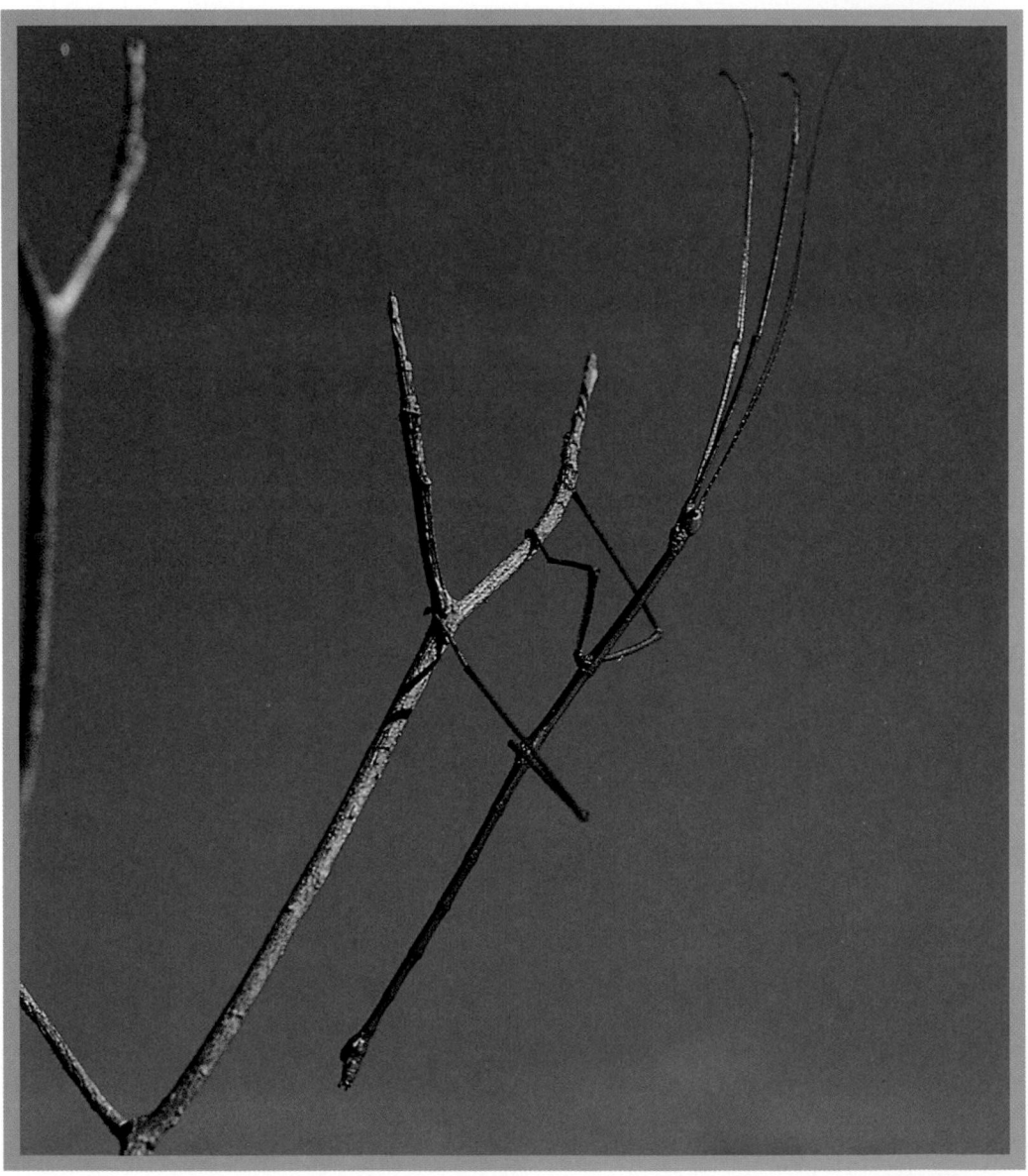

A walkingstick looks like the branches around it.

Animals, fish, reptiles, and even people use camouflage for hiding. When something looks like the objects around it, it is much harder to see. That is what camouflage is all about!

Why Do Animals Need Camouflage?

There are many reasons why animals hide. They often hide from their enemies. Some animals move around at night and sleep during the day. They need to stay hidden while they sleep.

This emperor moth has an eyespot on its wing to scare enemies.

Other animals hide so that they can be better hunters. Camouflage helps them sneak up on their dinner.

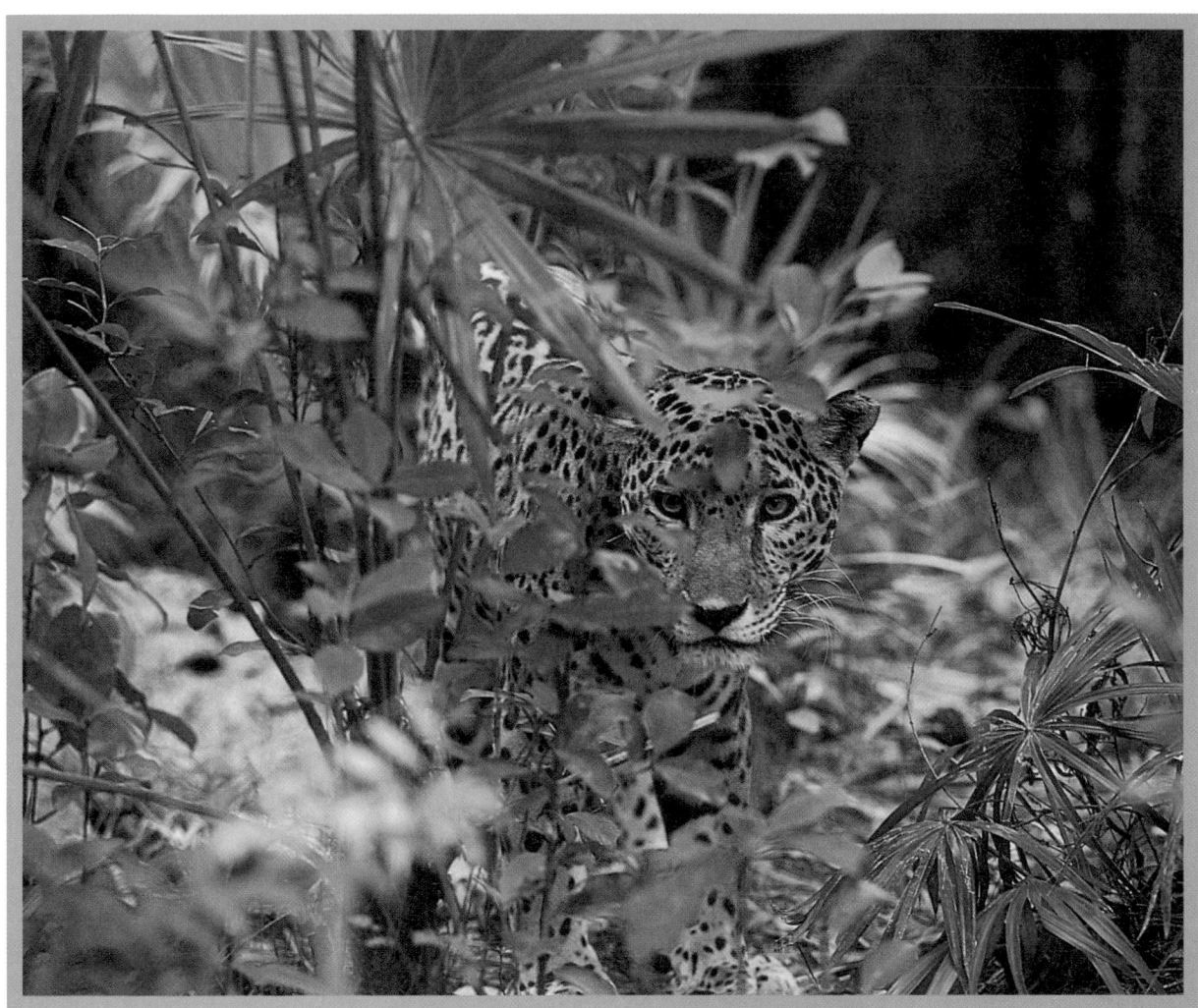

How Do Animals Use Camouflage?

Animals use camouflage in many different ways. Some use it to blend in with the objects around them. These objects are called surroundings. The *polar bear's* white coat blends in with its surroundings—the white snow. This color hides the bear when it is hunting for seals.

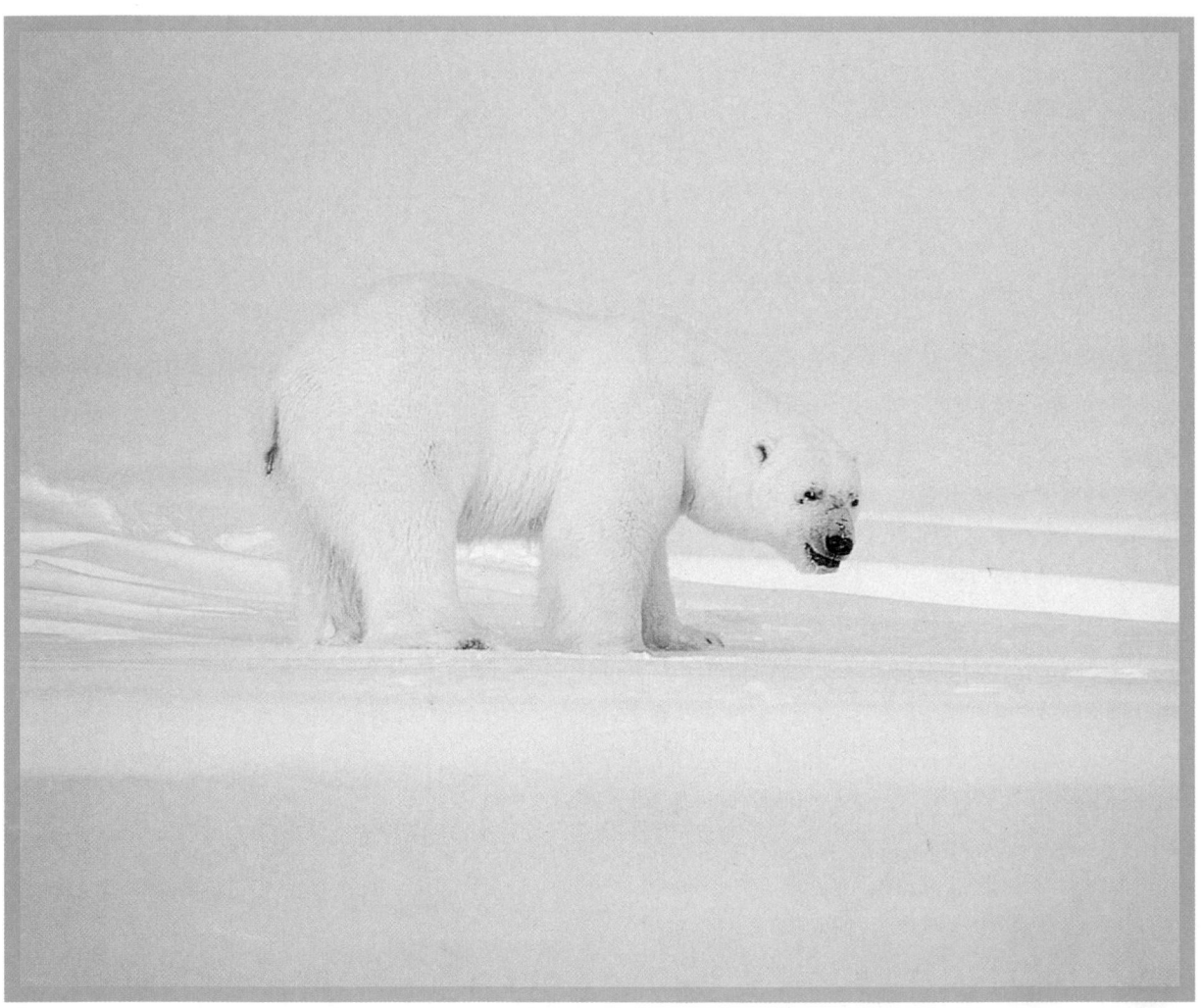

The white fur of this polar bear looks like the snow around it.

The *black bear's* dark coat helps it hide in dark trees and bushes.

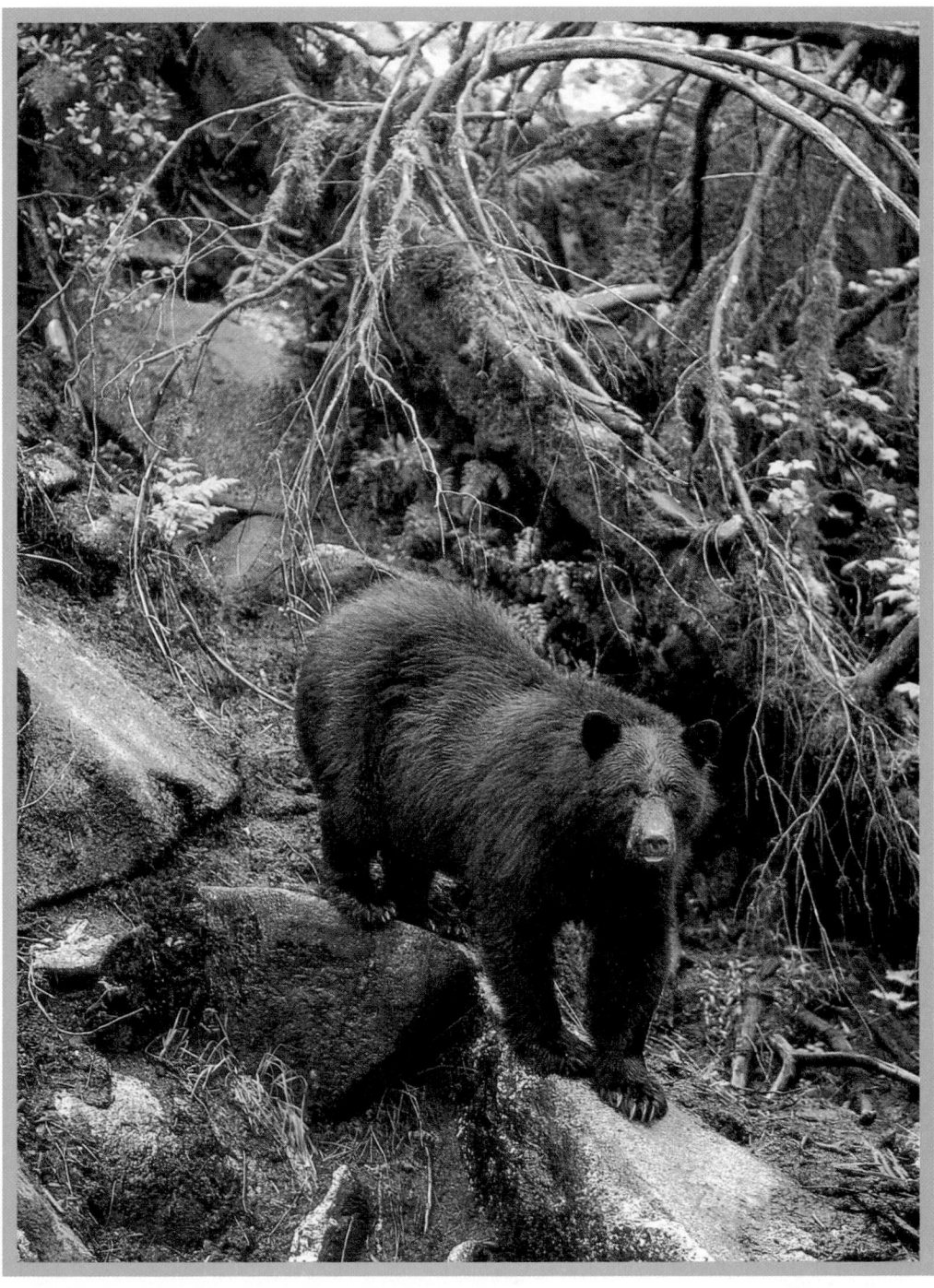

But what happens if an animal's surroundings are more than one color? Some animals have camouflage with more than one color, too!

Some fish have dark backs and white bellies. When a hungry bird looks into the dark water, the fish's dark back is hard to see. But to an enemy deeper in the water, the fish's white belly blends in with the bright sky.

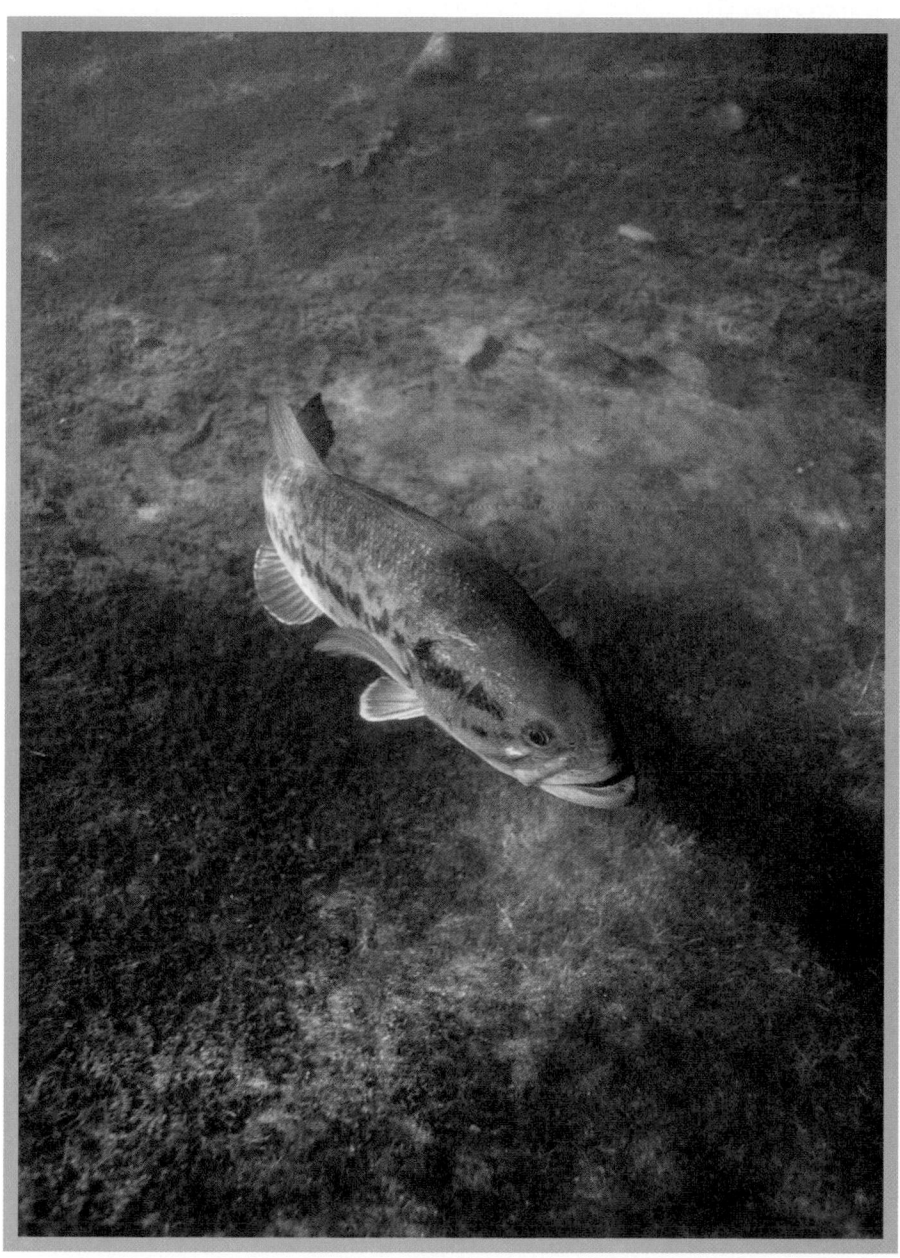

This large mouth bass has a dark back that matches the water.

Why Do Some Animals Change Color?

Sometimes an animal's surroundings change. Then the animal has to change color, too! That is the only way it can stay hidden. Some animals change color to match the season. The *snowshoe rabbit* changes color very slowly in the spring and fall.

In the winter, the snowshoe rabbit's fur is white like the snow. As the snow melts in the spring, the rabbit grows patches of brown fur. It looks just like patches of ground and melting snow.

This snowshoe rabbit has white fur to match the snow.

Then summer comes, and the ground is brown. The rabbit's fur grows brown to match. When fall comes, the rabbit starts to turn white again.

This baby snowshoe rabbit has brown fur in the spring.

Do All Animals Use Colors to Hide?

Some animals use designs, or patterns, instead of changing colors. Blending into a pattern is a good way to hide. When an animal's body looks like its surroundings, it is very hard to find.

A *fawn*, or baby deer, is too weak to run fast. But it can hide by lying still. The fawn's back is covered with dots. The dots look like spots of sunlight on the forest floor. If the fawn stays still, it is very hard to see.

Fawns like this one can blend into their surroundings.

Another animal that uses patterns to hide
is the *bittern*. This bird lives in marshes with
tall grass. The stripes on its feathers look
just like shadows in the grass.

This bittern has patterns that match the tall grass.

When the bittern is in danger, it makes itself even harder to find. It points its beak straight up and sways its body in the breeze. The bittern looks just like the blowing grass!

What Is Mimicry?

Some animals have a shape or color that looks like something else. This type of camouflage is called mimicry. Animals that use mimicry are good pretenders.

The *walkingstick* is one insect that uses mimicry. Its long, thin, bumpy body looks just like a small branch!

This walkingstick looks like a branch.

Walkingsticks can even change color with the seasons. In the spring, the tree's branches and leaves are green. The walkingstick is green, too. When the branches and leaves turn brown, the walkingstick turns brown to match.

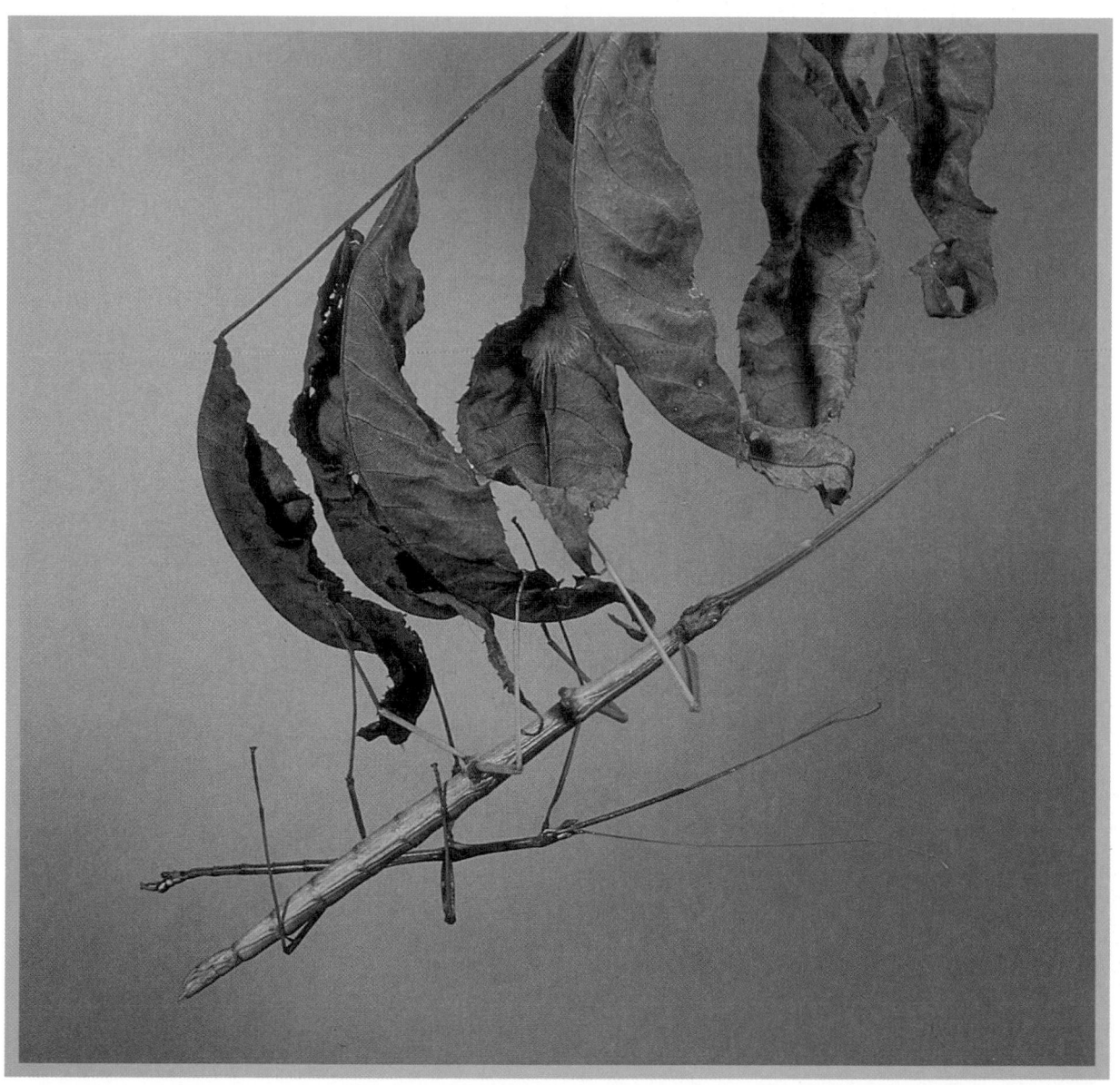

Some animals use other kinds of mimicry to fool their enemies. Some moths have large spots on their rear wings. The spots look just like eyes!

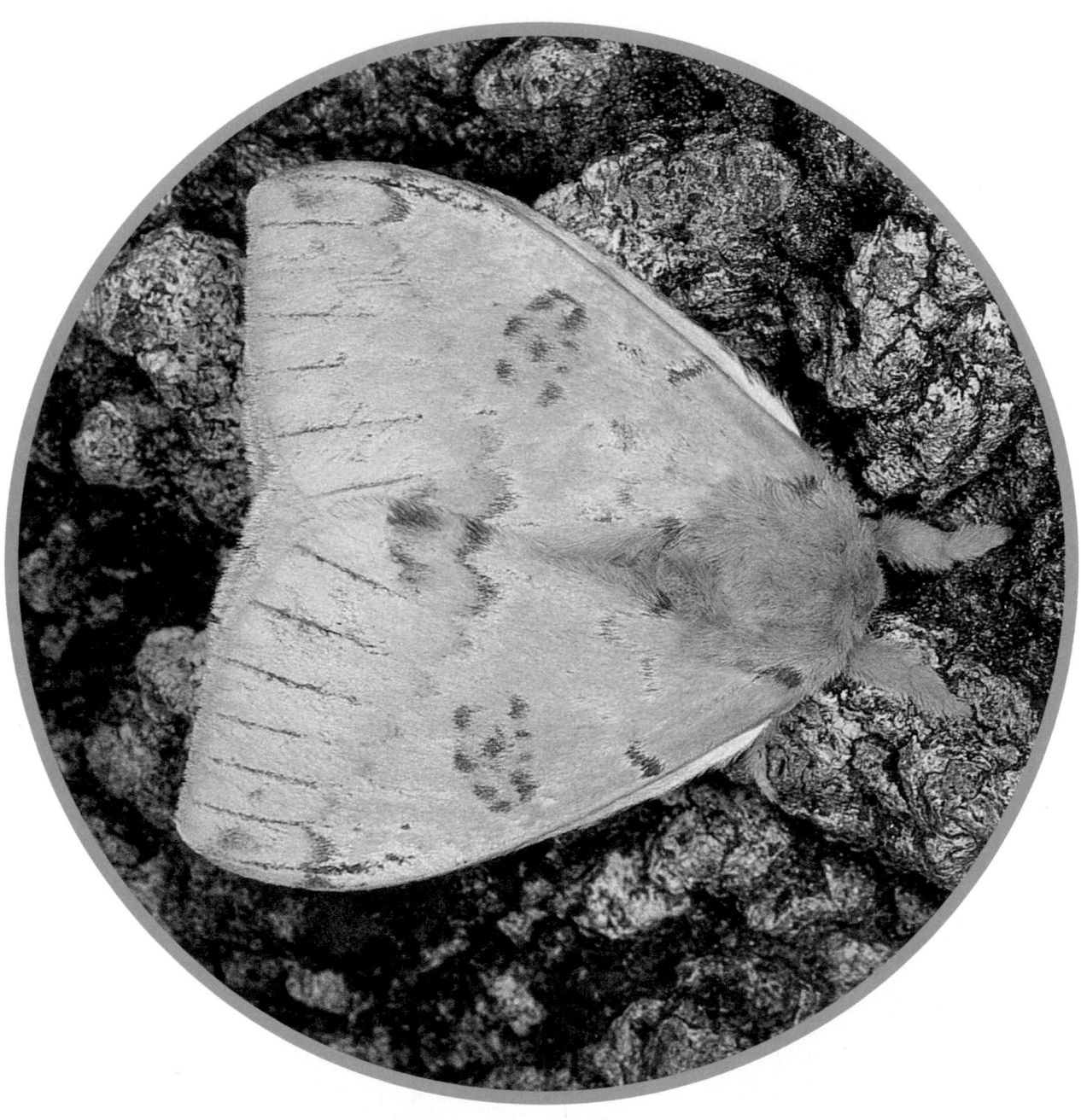

When the moth is resting, its front wings cover the spots. But when the moth senses danger, it lifts its front wings and shows the spots. If an enemy is afraid of the big "eyes," it will leave the moth alone.

The spots on this Io moth's wings look like eyes.

Some animals even make their own
costumes for camouflage. The *masked crab*
uses seaweed to make a costume.

This masked crab has used many things to make
its costume.

First the crab uses its claws to tear the seaweed into pieces. Then it puts each piece in its mouth and chews it until it is soft. The crab sticks the pieces of seaweed to itself. Little hooks on its shell and legs hold the seaweed in place.

From a rabbit that changes color to a crab in a seaweed costume, there are many kinds of camouflage. But each kind of camouflage has the same important job—to help animals hide.

This zale moth is hard to see because it looks like the tree trunk.

Now that you know some of their tricks, maybe you will see animals where you never saw them before. But you'll have to look very carefully, or you might be fooled!

Animal Camouflage

Concept Connections

Linking the Selection

Answer these questions in the Response Journal section of your Writer's Notebook.

- What are some different ways that animals use camouflage?

- Which animals were the most difficult to find in the photographs?

Exploring Concept Vocabulary

The concept word for this lesson is *pattern.* If you do not know what this word means, look it up in the dictionary. Answer these questions:

- What are three animals in the selection that use their *patterns* to hide?

- Do all animals use protective coloring or their *patterns* to hide for the same reason? Explain your answer.

In the Vocabulary section of your Writer's Notebook, write a sentence using the word *pattern* and one of the selection vocabulary words.

Expanding the Concept

Think about "Animal Camouflage" and the other unit selections. What have you learned about animal camouflage?

Try to use the word **pattern** as you talk about the characters and information in these selections. Then add new ideas about animal camouflage to the Concept/Question Board.

Meet the Author

Janet McDonnell came up with the idea for writing "Animal Camouflage" during a brainstorming session with publishers. Since she loves animals, she was excited to be given the chance to write about them. When she writes about a subject, she likes to research it very carefully. Sometimes she gets so much information that she cannot use it because the book can only be so long. Then her challenge is to get the ideas across in a clear and interesting way. *"My goal is to make the reader as excited about the topic as I am,"* she said.

Pronunciation Key

a as in **a**t

ā as in l**a**te

â as in c**a**re

ä as in f**a**ther

e as in s**e**t

ē as in m**e**

i as in **i**t

ī as in k**i**te

o as in **o**x

ō as in r**o**se

ô as in b**ou**ght and r**a**w

oi as in c**oi**n

o͝o as in b**oo**k

o͞o as in t**oo**

or as in f**or**m

ou as in **ou**t

u as in **u**p

ū as in **u**se

ûr as in t**ur**n; g**er**m, l**ear**n, f**ir**m, w**or**k

ə as in **a**bout, chick**e**n, penc**i**l, cann**o**n, circ**u**s

ch as in **ch**air

hw as in **wh**ich

ng as in ri**ng**

sh as in **sh**op

th as in **th**in

t͟h as in **th**ere

zh as in trea**s**ure

The mark (′) is placed after a syllable with a heavy accent, as in **chicken** (chik′ ən).

The mark (′) after a syllable shows a lighter accent, as in **disappear** (dis′ ə p ēr′).

Glossary

A

admire (ad mīr´) *v.* To be pleased with.

adobe (ə dō´ bē) *n.* A building made of brick or dried mud.

adrift (ə drift´) *adj.* Floating or moving without direction.

adventure (əd ven´ chər) *n.* A task or event that is likely to be exciting or dangerous.

amazement (ə māz´ mənt) *n.* Being very surprised and full of wonder.

amazing (ə mā´ zing) *adj.* Surprising; causing wonder.

amid (ə mid´) *prep.* In with; around; in the middle of.

anytime (en´ ē tīm´) *adv.* At any time.

Apache (ə pa´ chē) *adj.* Pertaining to a Native American group of the southwestern United States.

assistant (ə sis´ tənt) *n.* A helper; a person whose job is to help another person.

available (ə vā´ lə bəl) *adj.* Being in the area and ready to use.

avoid (ə void´) *v.* Stay away from.

B

ball (bôl) *n.* A large, fancy party at which people dance.

barely (bâr´ lē) *adv.* Only just; scarcely.

barnacles (bar´ nə kəlz) *n.* Small sea animals that have a shell and attach themselves to rocks, ship bottoms, and docks.

barnacles

C

beard (bērd) *n.* Hair on a chin.

beautiful (bū´ tə fəl) *adj.* Pleasing to look at, hear, or think about.

bizarre (bi zar´) *adj.* Very unusual looking.

blend (blend) *v.* Mix together so as not to be seen.

bloom (bloom) *n.* A large group of plankton on the ocean surface.

boring (bôr ing) *adj.* To make tired or restless by being dull.

brow (brou) *n.* Area including the eyebrows and forehead.

bulletin board (bu´ lə tən bord) *n.* A place on a wall for messages and other information.

butterfly (bu´ tûr flī´) *n.* An insect with a thin body and four large, often brightly colored wings. Butterflies fly in the daytime.

calabash (ka´ lə bash´) *n.* A gourd with a hard shell that can be made into a dipper.

calm (käm) *adj.* Not excited or nervous; quiet.

camouflage (kam´ ə fläzh) *adj.* Hard to see because it looks the same as the area around it.

cane (kān) *n.* A stick to help a person in walking.

cattail (kat´ tāl´) *n.* A tall reedy plant with a fuzzy brown top that grows in very wet areas.

cattail

cautiously (kô´ shəs lē) *adv.* With care; watching out for danger.

ceiling (sē´ ling) *n.* The top of a room.

cellar (sel´ ər) *n.* A room underground.

chance (chans) *n.* A time for one to do something.

chatter (cha´ tər) *v.* To click together quickly.

chrysalis (kris´ ə lis) *n.* The protective covering around the butterfly larva when it is in the stage of changing into butterfly.

cinder (sin´ dər) *n.* A small bit of coal or wood that has been burned until it is black.

clearing (klēr´ ing) *n.* In a forest, a piece of land with no trees or bushes.

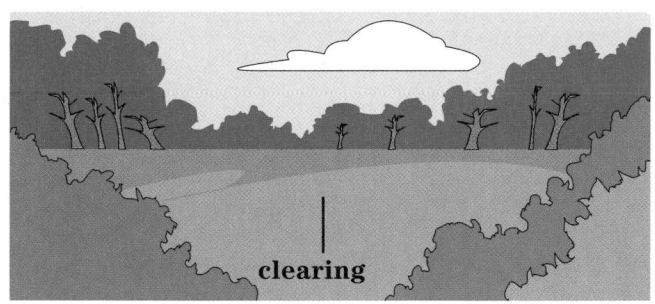

clearing

clever (kle´ vər) *adj.* Very smart.

coachman (kōch´ mən) *n.* A person who drives a carriage.

cobbler (kob´ lər) *n.* A person who makes and repairs shoes.

coloration (kə´ lə rā´ shən) *n.* The way something is colored.

concrete torpedo (kon´ krēt tor pē´ dō) *n.* A heavy block of stone used to hit something hard enough to make it break apart.

costume (kos´ tōōm´) *n.* Something put on to change the way one looks.

cot (kot) *n.* A small bed that usually can be folded.

courthouse (kort´ hous´) *n.* A building with courtrooms and offices.

court (kort´) *v.* Trying to find a mate.

crane (krān) *n.* A bird with a long neck, beak, and legs that lives near water.

crane

crane (krān) *v.* To stretch out the neck in order to see better.

creature (krē´ chər) *n.* Any animal that is alive.

crept (krept) *v.* A past tense of

creep (krēp) *v.* To move slowly and quietly.

crumpled (krum′ pəld) *adj.* Crushed and bent out of shape.

D

decorate (de′ kə rāt′) *v.* To add designs or pictures to make something look better.

delicious (di lish′ əs) *adj.* Pleasing or delightful to the taste or smell.

department (di pärt′ mənt) *n.* A single area of a store; a part of a store where one type of item is sold.

design (di zīn′) *v.* Make by following a plan.

diamond (dī′ mənd) *n.* A mineral that consists of pure carbon in the form of a clear or pale crystal. It is the hardest natural material known.

dine (dīn) *v.* To eat food.

disappear (dis′ ə pēr′) *v.* To no longer be seen.

disguise (dis gīz′) *n.* Anything that hides something from view.

don (don) *v.* To put on, like clothes.

donation (dō nā′ shən) *n.* Something given to a person or group.

drab (drab) *adj.* Plain and without color.

drenched (drenched) *v.* To make something completely wet.

drift (drift) *v.* To move because of a current of air or water.

droop (drōop) *v.* To hang or sink down.

drowsy (drou′ zē) *adj.* Feeling sleepy.

E

eager (ē′ gər) *adj.* Looking forward to doing something.

elves (elvz) *n.* The plural of **elf:** A small fairy who sometimes plays tricks.

enemy (en´ ə mē) *n.* Animal that might cause harm.

enormous (i nôr´ məs) *adj.* Huge; very big.

escalator (es´ kə lā´ tər) *n.* A moving stairway.

exciting (eks sīt´ ing) *adj.* Causing excitement.

exclaim (iks klām´) *v.* To cry out suddenly.

F

fade (fād) *v.* Lose some of the color.

fasten (fas´ ən) *v.* To attach firmly.

fawn (fôn) *n.* A young deer.

fig (fig) *n.* A sweet fruit of a shrub or small tree that grows in warm regions. Figs have many tiny seeds, and are often preserved by drying.

fig

finally (fī´ nəl lē) *adv.* At the end; at last.

flick (flik) *v.* To move in a rapid or jerky way.

forgave (fər gāv´) *v.* The past tense of **forgive**: To pardon; to excuse.

froth (frôth) *n.* Bubbles formed in a liquid; foamy liquid.

G

gasp (gasp) *v.* To breathe in gulps with the mouth wide open.

glare (glâr) *v.* To look at with anger.

glide (glīd) *v.* To move in a smooth and steady way.

glisten (gli´ sən) *v.* To shine or sparkle.

glossy (glo´ sē) *adj.* Having a shine or luster.

goddess (god´ is) *n.* A female god.

gown (goun) *n.* A woman's dress, often fancy.

granary (grā´ nə rē) *n.* A building in which grains, such as corn or wheat, are stored.

> **Pronunciation Key:** a**t**; l**ā**te; c**â**re; f**ä**ther; s**e**t; m**ē**; **it**; k**ī**te; **ox**; r**ō**se; **ô** in b**ou**ght; c**oi**n; b**oo**k; t**oo**; f**or**m; **out**; **up**; **use**; t**û**rn; **ə** sound in **a**bout, chick**e**n, penc**i**l, cann**o**n, circ**u**s; **ch**air; **hw** in **wh**ich; ri**ng**; **sh**op; **th**in; **th**ere; **zh** in trea**s**ure.

greedy (grē´ dē) *adj.* A very great and selfish desire for more than one's share.

grip (grip) *v.* To take hold of firmly and tightly.

grotesque (grō tesk´) *adj.* Odd or unusual looking.

guest (gest) *n.* A customer in a restaurant, hotel, or similar place.

guinea fowl (gi´ nē foul) *n.* An African bird that has a bare neck and head.

guinea fowl

gulp (gulp) *n.* To swallow large amounts of something all at one time.

H

handsome (han´ səm) *adj.* Having a pleasing appearance.

herd (hûrd) *n.* A group of animals.

herd

host (hōst) *n.* The person who is taking care of guests.

hover (hu´ vər) *v.* To stay in one place while in the air.

howling (houl ing) *v.* To make a loud, wailing cry.

huddle (hud´ l) *v.* To crowd together; to wrap up tightly in.

hue (hū) *n.* Color.

I

ice-breaker (īs´ brā´ kər) *n.* A ship used to break a channel through ice.

ice-breaker

ice-pole (īs´ pōl) *n.* A metal pole with a pointed end used to chip ice.

imitator (i´ mə tā´ tər) *n.* One who copies something or someone.

incredible (in kred´ ə bəl) *adj.* Beyond belief.

Inuit (i´ nōō wət) *n.* People native to the northwestern part of North America and Arctic.

invincible (in´ vin´ sə bəl) *adj.* So strong that it cannot be beaten or broken.

invisible (in viz´ ə bəl) *adj.* Not able to be seen.

K

katydid (kā´ tē did´) *n.* A large, green grasshopper.

katydid

kingdom (king´ dəm) *n.* A country that is ruled by a king or a queen.

L

lad (lad) *n.* A male child; boy.

lap (lap) *v.* To drink by pulling liquid into the mouth with the tongue.

larva (lar´ və) *n.* The newly hatched form of some insects and other animals without backbones. A larva has a soft body that looks like a worm and has no wings. A caterpillar is the larva of a moth or butterfly, and a grub is the larva of a beetle.

lean (lēn) *v.* To sit with one's back resting against something.

leather (leth´ ər) *n.* The skin of an animal after it has been tanned, or softened; for use in making shoes and other items.

librarian (lī brâr´ ē ən) *n.* A person who is in charge of or works in a library.

library card (lī´ brâr´ ē kard) *n.* A card which lets you borrow library books.

lurk (lûrk) *v.* To move slowly and quietly without being noticed.

M

manner (ma´ nər) *n.* A way of acting or behaving.

marigold (mâr i gōld) *n.* A garden plant that bears yellow, orange, or red flowers in summer.

marigold

marsh (marsh) *n.* Low, wet land. Grasses and reeds grow in marshes.

meadow (med´ ō) *n.* A field of grass.

midnight (mid´ nīt´) *n.* Twelve o´clock at night; the middle of the night.

mimicry (mim´ i krē) *n.* Camouflage that makes an animal look like another kind of animal.

mistake (mi stāk´) *v.* Something that is not correctly done, said, or thought; error.

mystery (mis´ tə rē) *n.* Something that is not or cannot be known, explained, or understood.

N

natural (na´ chə rəl) *adj.* Acting on information one is born with.

nearsighted (nēr´ sī´ tid) *adj.* Not able to see things far away.

nectar (nek´ tûr) *n.* The sweet liquid formed in flowers. Bees use nectar to make honey.

nimble (nim´ bəl) *adj.* Able to move easily; light on one's feet.

O

olympiad (ō lim´ pē ad) *n.* A great contest.

ordeal (or dēl´) *v.* A stressful time or event.

overalls (ō´ vər ôlz´) *n.* Loose trousers with a bib front and straps at the shoulders.

overjoyed (ō´ vûr joid´) *adj.* Extremely happy.

P

pack-ice (pak´ īs´) *n.* Sea ice that forms when pieces of floating ice get crushed together.

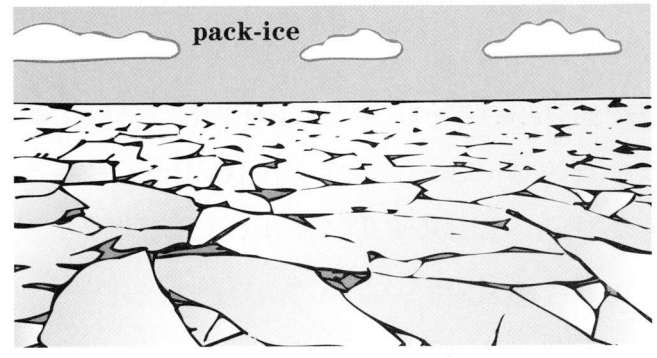
pack-ice

page (pāj) *n.* A boy servant.

palace (pal´ is) *n.* A large, fancy house; the home of a king and queen.

parlor (par´ lər) *n.* A room for visiting with friends.

particular (pər ti´ kyə lər) *adj.* Being one single thing.

patient (pā´ shənt) *adj.* Calm; willing to wait; able to put up with a bad situation without complaining.

patterns (pat´ ərnz) *n.* Repeated shapes or colors on an animal.

perform (pər form´) *v.* To act, sing, or dance in front of others.

> **Pronunciation Key: at**; l**ā**te; c**â**re; f**ä**ther; s**e**t; m**ē**; **i**t; k**ī**te; **o**x; r**ō**se; **ô** in b**ou**ght; c**oi**n; b**oo**k; t**oo**; f**o**rm; **ou**t; **u**p; **u**se; t**û**rn; **ə** sound in ab**ou**t, chick**e**n, penc**i**l, cann**o**n, circ**u**s; **ch**air; **hw** in **wh**ich; ri**ng**; **sh**op; **th**in; **th**ere; **zh** in trea**s**ure.

perspire (pər spīr´) v. To sweat.

persuade (pər swād´) v. To convince someone to do or believe something.

plaid (plad) n. A pattern of overlapping squares, rectangles, and lines.

plaid

plankton (plangk´ tən) n. A kind of very small plant life in a body of water.

plight (plīt) n. A bad situation.

plunge (plunj) v. To dive down into the water.

polish (po´ ləsh) v. To make smooth and shiny by rubbing.

polka dot (pō´ kə dot´) n. A pattern of solid colored circles.

praying mantis (prā´ ing man´ tis) n. Large, green insect that holds its front legs as if praying.

praying mantis

pretender (prē tend ûr) v. One who gives a false show.

promptly (prompt´ lē) adv. Quickly.

protect (prə tekt´) v. To keep from harm.

protective (prə tek´ tiv) adj. Keeps out of danger or away from harm.

prying (prī´ ing) adj. Being nosey.

pteranodon (tə ra´ nə don) n. A flying dinosaur.

Q

quickly (kwik´ lē) adv. Thinking, learning, or reacting easily and rapidly.

R

raid (rād) *n.* A sudden entering to take something.

ridge (rij) *n.* The long and narrow upper part of something.

reply (ri plī´) *v.* To answer.

rounds (roundz) *n.* The same trip taken over and over; a route taken that begins each time in the same place.

S

search (sûrch) *v.* To look for.

scent (sent) *n.* Smell.

scramble (skram´ bəl) *v.* To move or climb quickly.

serve (serv) *v.* To bring food to.

shimmer (shim´ ûr) *v.* To shine with a faint, flickering light; glimmer.

shoemaker (shoo´ mā´ kər) *n.* A person who makes or repairs shoes.

shopper (shop´ ər) *n.* A person who is looking for things to buy.

shrubby (shru´ bē) *adj.* Filled out with leaves and limbs; bushy.

sigh (sī) *v.* To let out a loud breath.

sky-crane (skī´ krān) *n.* A machine that uses cables to lift and move heavy objects.

slink (slingk) *v.* To move quietly, slowly, and close to the ground; to creep.

slither (slith´ ûr) *v.* To slide or glide like a snake.

sneaky (snē´ kē) *adj.* Trying to keep from being seen.

sniff (snif) *v.* To smell; to draw a short breath up the nose.

snoopy (snoo´ pē) *adj.* Looking for or prowling.

sofa (sō´ fə) *n.* A couch with a back and two arms.

spatter (spa´ tər) *v.* To splash with small drops.

spied (spīd) *v.* To notice.

splutter (splu´ tər) *v.* To say with a splashing sound.

sporting (spor´ ting) *v.* Showing.

squid (skwid) *n.* A sea animal with a tube-shaped body and ten arms.

squid

stacks (staks) *n.* Piles formed by putting books on top of each other.

stalk (stôk) *n.* The main stem of a plant.

stare (stâr) *v.* To look very hard or very long with the eyes wide open.

steadies (sted´ ēs) *adj.* Firm in movement or position; not shaky.

steamer trunk (stē´ mər trungk) *n.* A big, strong box with a lid used for storage.

steamer trunk

steep (stēp) *adj.* Almost straight up-and-down.

stranger (strān´ jûr) *n.* A person whom one does not know.

stubby (stu´ bē) *adj.* Short and thick.

supermarket (sōō´ pər mär´ kət) *n.* A store in which a person can choose food and household items to buy.

surface (sûr´ fəs) *n.* The top part of something.—*v.* To come up to the surface.

surroundings (sə roun´ dingz) *n.* The objects around an animal.

swoop (swōōp) *v.* To fly down then back up quickly.

T

tasseled (ta´ səld) *adj.* Looking like a tassel, which is a bunch of strings tied at one end.

temperature (tem´ pə chər´) *n.* A measure of how warm or cold something is.

tender (ten´ dər) *adj.* Soft and gentle.

thorny (thor´ nē) *adj.* Having a sharp point on a branch or stem.

top hat (top´ hat´) *n.* A man's hat that has a tall top shaped like a tube.

top hat

toppled (to´ pəld) *adj.* Overturned.

transform (trans´ form) *v.* To change outward appearance.

trout (trout) *n.* A long bony fish.

trudge (truj) *v.* To walk with great effort.

tutoring (tōō´ tər ing) *n.* Helping others with school work.

twitch (twich) *v.* To move with a jerk.

U

unaware (ən´ ə wâr´) *adv.* Not knowing what is happening.

unusual (un ū´ zhōō əl) *adj.* Not usual, common, or ordinary; rare.

W

wakeful (wāk´ fəl) *adj.* Restless, not able to sleep.

wand (wond) *n.* A magic rod; a stick that is used for magic.

wariest (wâr´ ē əst) *adj.* Superlative of **wary**: Having a feeling that danger may be near; watching for danger.

watchman (woch´ mən) *n.* A man whose job is to guard property.

> **Pronunciation Key: a**t; l**ā**te; c**â**re; f**ä**ther; s**e**t; m**ē**; **i**t; k**ī**te; **o**x; r**ō**se; **ô** in b**ou**ght; **coi**n; b**ŏŏ**k; t**ōō**; f**o**rm; **ou**t; **u**p; **u**se; t**û**rn; **ə** sound in about, chicken, pencil, cannon, circus; **ch**air; **hw** in **wh**ich; ri**ng**; **sh**op; **th**in; **th**ere; **zh** in treasure.

waterspout (wô´ tər spout´) *n.* A stream of water that shoots from a whale's blowhole when it comes to the surface for air.

wedged (wejd) *v.* To drive, push, or crowd.

whir (hwûr) *v.* To fly quickly, making a noise with wings.

whirlwind (hwûrl´ wind´) *n.* Wind that moves in a circle with great force.

wily (wī´ lē) *adj.* Sly or crafty.

Y

yip (yip) *v.* To make a short high-pitched sound.

Photo Credits

11, ©Tom & Pat Leeson/DRK Photo; **22 (t),** file photo, **(b)** ©SYS, Japan; **80,** Albert Whitman Company; **82,** The National Museum of American Art, Smithsonian Institution, Washinton, DC. Gift of S.C. Johnson & Son, Inc./ Art Resource, NY; **83 (t),** Christie's Images, **(b)** The Metropolitan Museum of Art, Arthur Hoppock Hearn Fund, 1913. Photograph ©1988 The Metropolitan Museum of Art; **104 (t),** ©Arte Publico Press, **(b)** ©Bernd Noble; **118 (t),** file photo, **(b)** Jose Aruego; **136 (t),** Scholastic, **(b)** file photo; **154, 176,** file photo; **178,** The Metropolitan Museum of Art, Rogers Fund, 1930. Photograph ©1979 The Metropolitan Museum of Art; **179 (t),** University of Pennsylvania Museum, Philadelphia, neg # T4-171c, **(b)** The Museum of Fine Arts, Houston; The John A. and Audrey Jones Beck Collection; **196,** file photo; **220,** The Times; **234 (t),** Adri Coen, **(b)** Lane Yerkes; **250,** Scholastic; **264 (t),** Craig Kee Strete, **(b)** Jose Aruego; **294,** The Norton Simon Foundation, Pasadena, California; **295 (t),** ©Tom Amedis, **(b)** The National Museum of Women in the Arts, Washington, DC. Gift of Deidre Busenberg and the Artist; **332,** Barbara Knutson; **334,** Darrell Gulin/DRK Photo; **335,** Tom Till/DRK Photo; **336,** Fred Bruemmer/DRK Photo; **337,** ©M.C. Chamberlain/DRK Photo; **338,** James P. Rowan/DRK Photo; **339,** ©Tom & Pat Leeson/DRK Photo; **340,** Andy Rouse/DRK Photo; **341,** Pat & Tom Leeson/Photo Researchers, Inc.; **342,** C.C. Lockwood/Animals Animals; **343,** Larry Mishkar/Dembinsky Photo Associates; **344,** Rod Planck/ Photo Researchers, Inc.; **345,** Wayne Lankinen/DRK Photo; **346,** Stan Wayman/Photo Researchers, Inc.; **347,** Leonard Lee Rue III//DRK Photo; **348,** Wayne Lankinen/DRK Photo; **349,** Gary R. Zahm/DRK Photo; **350,** Gilbert S. Grant/Photo Researchers, Inc.; **351,** Joe McDonald/DRK Photo; **352,** M.H. Sharp/Photo Researchers, Inc.; **353,** Ray Coleman/Photo Researchers, Inc.; **354,** Bruce Watkins/Animals Animals; **355,** Tom McHugh/Photo Researchers, Inc.; **356,** John Bova/Photo Researchers, Inc.; **357,** David M. Schleser/Photo Researchers, Inc.; **358,** Janet McDonnell.

Art Acknowledgments

Unit 1 (Sharing Stories) Bill Ogden
Unit 2 (Kindness) Sucie Stevenson
Unit 3 (Look Again) Dara Goldman